4° "Immersione totale » nel lusso
e nel gusto.
1919

5° Geometrie del 1919 in anteprima
sull'arte Op.

6° Vanno senza fine al di sopra delle cose,
non guardano dove vanno,
ma non ha importanza,
sono alla moda.
1926

MODE *series directed by Maria Luisa Frisa*

Vittoria Caterina Caratozzolo

# IRENE BRIN

## Italian style in fashion

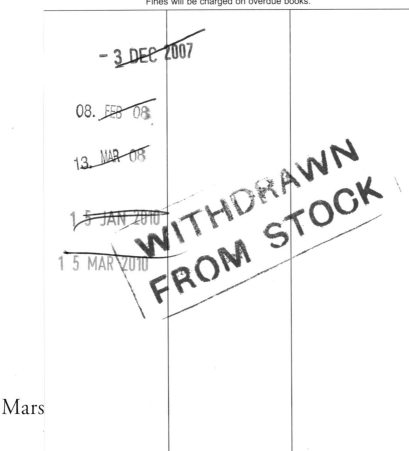
Mars

This book stems from a reworking of the thesis written at the conclusion of a research doctorate in the History of Women's Writing at "La Sapienza" University in Rome. I would like to express my sincere gratitude to my supervisor, Marina Zancan, and to the Faculty Board. For providing me with access to much of the documentary material that has been indispensable to the realization of this book, I would like to thank: Maria Vittoria Marini Clarelli, superintendent of the Galleria Nazionale d'Arte Moderna (GNAM); the director Angela Andreina Rorro, along with Claudia Palma and Stefania Navarra, in charge of the Archivio della Galleria dell'Obelisco and the Fondi Storici of the GNAM; Iaia and Natalia Indrimi, in charge of the Archivio Irene Brin and the Archivio dell'Obelisco at the Associazione Culturale La Centrale dell'Arte. My special thanks go to: Giorgio Roberto Rubin and Patrizia Sabatini for the generous assistance they gave me in my consultation of the collections of Bellezza and Harper's Bazaar that used to belong to Irene Brin and are now in the library of the Accademia di Costume e di Moda in Rome; and to Rossella Caruso for her invaluable suggestions.

translation: Huw Evans

graphic design: Alessandro Gori.Laboratorium

cover: Irene Brin, photo Ghergo
inside cover and inside back cover:
Illustrations by Brunetta. From Brunetta, *Metamorfosi*, Milan: Giorgio Lucini Editore, 1968.
Courtesy Fondi Storici, Galleria Nazionale d'Arte Moderna, Rome

Fondazione Pitti Discovery apologizes and is available
if any photographic credits have been unintentionally omitted

© 2006 by Fondazione Pitti Discovery
www.pittimmagine.com

© 2006 by Marsilio Editori ® s.p.a.
in Venice
www.marsilioeditori.it

First edition: November 2006
ISBN 88-317-8958

Distributed in the UK and Europe by
Windsor Books
The Boundary
Wheatley Road
Garsington Oxford OX44 9EJ
tel 01865361122 fax 01865361133

Distributed throughout the rest of the world by
Rizzoli International Publications
300 Park Avenue South,
New York, NY 10010
tel 2123873400 fax 212383535
www.rizzoliusa.com

Printed by Grafiche Nardin, Ca' Savio - Cavallino - Treporti (Venice)
for Marsilio Editori® spa in Venice

# CONTENTS

# 4 Minds on Fashion

**Carmel Snow**

The fashion reporting in HARPER'S BAZAAR has always been liberally international in outlook. This is not surprising, since the magazine has editors with an innate flair for fashion in each of the four capitals where it is created. The other day, a transatlantic network broadcast in the United States a HARPER'S BAZAAR talk, contributed to from New York, London, Paris and Rome, and the four minds were bent on one subject—fashion as it manifests itself in the four countries. Here, photographed, are the four speakers. ● Carmel Snow, American editor-in-chief, is the greatest single influence on fashion in the United States: her report from the Paris Collections is read and followed all over the States, and the clothes she chooses for the magazine are soon adapted for American stores. In 1949, Mrs. Snow was made a Chevalier of the Legion of Honour, for her influence in re-establishing the prestige of French design in the U.S.A. . . . ● Eileen Dickson, editor of the British edition, maintains that fashion, now a serious business everywhere, should be fun too. She herself always wears clothes that are

**Eileen Dickson**

**Irene Brin**

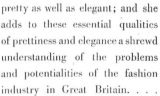
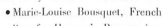
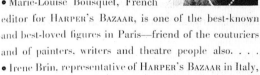

pretty as well as elegant; and she adds to these essential qualities of prettiness and elegance a shrewd understanding of the problems and potentialities of the fashion industry in Great Britain. . . . ● Marie-Louise Bousquet, French

**Marie-Louise Bousquet**

editor for HARPER'S BAZAAR, is one of the best-known and best-loved figures in Paris—friend of the couturiers and of painters, writers and theatre people also. . . . ● Irene Brin, representative of HARPER'S BAZAAR in Italy, is a woman of distinctive elegance and a scintillating talent for journalism which flares out in a dozen directions. Like Mme Bousquet, she frequents the artists of her country; knows the designers, and is active in helping to arrange their openings.

PHOTOGRAPHS BY LOUISE
DAHL-WOLFE, KUBLIN, TABARD

"4 Minds on Fashion," photo by Louise Dahl-Wolfe, Kublin, Tabard. From *Harper's Bazaar UK*, March 1955. Courtesy Accademia di Costume e di Moda, Rome. Donated by Irene Brin

# MISS, MAY I TAKE YOUR PICTURE?

*My love of clothes interests me profoundly only it is not love;*
*& what it is I must discover.*
(Virginia Woolf)

*I understood very little about fashion.*
(Irene Brin)

"Revealing a Genius Yes, a Secret Love No"[1] was the resolute title of
one of Irene Brin's last articles. She had written it to launch the first
issue of *Harper's Bazaar Italia*, brought out in January 1969 as an
offshoot of the classic *Harper's Bazaar*: a magazine for which she had
been working as Rome editor since 1952, representing its main link
with the Italian fashion world. The new publication, which operated
alongside its parent in a synergetic relationship between the
journalists in Italy and the editorial staff in New York, was a tangible
sign of the maturity attained by Italian fashion. After so many years
of work, commencing after the war, it was a timely recognition of its
importance: at last the "genius" of Italian fashion, at that point fully

"revealed," had been assigned the role it deserved as a leading actor
on the variegated international stage.

From the mid-forties up until the end of the sixties, Irene Brin made
a fundamental contribution to the promotion of Italian creativity,
against a backdrop of profound social and cultural change, and not in
Italy alone. With the years of Fascist repression over, the journalist
had finally been able to draw freely on her own cosmopolitan
background, finding in it a resource that could be placed at the
service of the country during its reconstruction. A background that
had in any case never been completely censored: even at the height of
the regime's autarkic culture, between 1939 and 1943, she had
shown her disdain for the model of woman as mother and mistress of
the home championed by Fascist propaganda by proposing some of
the most stimulating products of international culture to the readers
of the *Almanacco della donna italiana* in her column "I libri che ho
letto" ("Books I Have Read"). The keen interest that she expressed in
European and American literature, the efforts she made to popularize
the works of woman writers like Virginia Woolf, Gertrude Stein and
Rebecca West, was accompanied by a desire to keep constantly
abreast of lifestyles on the other side of the Alps and the ocean.
Subscribing to the most representative international fashion
magazines, like *Vogue* and *Harper's Bazaar*, Irene Brin showed herself,
right from the beginning of her career as a journalist, to be acute in
her discernment of which elements of Italian fashion were most
appreciated abroad. The dialectical nature of her gifts for
communication allowed her, as a journalist and commentator, to
make a considerable contribution to the creation of an Italian culture
of fashion: it was a constructive comparison, the one she carried out,
that gradually increased Italian creators' awareness of the real value of
their sartorial inventions. Anticipating what is going to be discussed
in the following pages, and finding a formula to sum it up, we can
say here that the key feature of the "Irene Brin viewpoint" was her
constant, meticulous and painstaking focus on the necessary
relationship that exists between the garment and the accessory, on the
one hand, and the specific cultural situation that promotes those
objects at the level of production and consumption, on the other. A
situation that she saw, and that she taught us to see as well, as inevitably

steeped in the value of the "place": of the *genius loci* that would turn out to be so attractive to the foreign customer. And so, eschewing any temptation to indulge in local color and folklore, Italian fashion design would increasingly project itself, after the war, into that transnational and transcultural dimension that it is now fully acknowledged to possess by the most up-to-date analyses carried out in the realm of fashion studies. So not only must the article written for *Harper's Bazaar Italia* on the threshold of the seventies have represented for its author – nearing the end of her career and her life – a confirmation of the correctness of the intuitions she had followed up till then, but for us today it remains a precious testimony of just how farsighted was her view and interpretation of the fashion phenomenon.

The publication of the Italian edition of *Harper's Bazaar* provided Irene Brin with an official opportunity to reexamine the magazine's evolution over the course of the slightly more than a hundred years since its appearance on the American market. She credited the "doyen of all luxury international magazines"[2] with having made no small contribution to modifying the lifestyles of the Western world, in ways that were only in appearance "facetious, superficial or even lazy,"[3] but in reality capable of deeply influencing the taste of broad strata of society. Conceived by editors and writers belonging to the American Social Register and the European *Almanach de Gotha*, the sophisticated magazine had initially been aimed at women from the restricted circle of New York "patricians," of "refined Boston Quakers or opulent Chicago millionaires,"[4] all insatiably on the lookout for new ways of decorating their homes, their gardens and their own persons. An elitist perspective, to be sure, but one not devoid, nevertheless, of a subtle form of authority over its first haughty and mistrustful readers, called on to take cognizance not only of the latest dictates of fashion but also of the emergence of a new social go-between, the authoritative figure of the fashion journalist and commentator. When Carmel Snow had become the editor of *Harper's Bazaar*, a series of slow but constant changes had modified the look and function of the magazine. The intention was to transform the journal into an eclectic medium of communication capable of grasping the multiple aspects of the fashion phenomenon and of registering their presence within the contemporary cultural scene.

This evolution had entailed the enlistment of prestigious art
directors, commencing with Brodovitch, and a galaxy of
photographers like Hoyningen-Huene, Cartier-Bresson, Avedon,
Penn, Dahl-Wolfe and Hiro: all engaged in creatively constructing
the visual heritage of fashion. At the same time, the magazine found
itself in a position to promote promising figures in the literary world,
showing perspicacity in their identification. Writers like the then
unknown Pasternak, Carson McCullers at the outset of her career,
Nathalie Sarraute and Pier Paolo Pasolini were all given a platform in
the pages of *Harper's Bazaar*. Yet the burst of enthusiasm with which
those authors were presented to the world was followed by an equally
sudden loss of affection for them. Nor was there anything surprising
about this: in the world of fashion any sort of fervor is doomed to
melt away "at the first sign of fatigue."[5]
This is what would happen to the "philosopher" Marshall McLuhan:
that was how Irene Brin described the founder of the science of
media. Just a few months earlier, in April 1968, McLuhan had
published his article "Fashion is the Medium" in *Harper's Bazaar*. The
editorial staff had asked the Canadian theorist – who at that time was
teaching a course entitled "Understanding Media" at Fordham
University's Center for Communications in New York – to write an
article that, in the light of his latest ideas about the science of
communication, would usher in the second century of the magazine's
publication with a completely new perspective on the phenomenon of
fashion. The final version of the essay took the form of a sort of
collage of images and text put together by the anthropologist Ted
Carpenter, a friend of McLuhan and his close collaborator during the
year he spent at Fordham University. The feature explored the
dimension of a new female image, simultaneously brought into focus
by the interaction between the visual experiments of the
photographic techniques of Hiro and Guy Bourdin, the new styles of
clothing and McLuhan's theories on fashion as a means of social
participation: "Fashion is not a way of being informed or aware, but a
way of being *with* it."[6] Like the electronic media and in a way that
was similar to what used to happen in the tribal world, fashion again
plunged the person "into the embrace of the group"[7] bringing him or
her into a space of polysensorial and synesthetic interaction, no longer

modeled on the supremacy of the eye over the other senses. The hard-edge design of late sixties fashion was interpreted by McLuhan as a repudiation of the values of uniformity, linearity and consistency connected with a way of life characterized predominantly by an abstract visual order. To conjure up the different approach to perception so incisively stimulated by fashion, McLuhan suggested to the readers of *Harper's Bazaar* that they put themselves in the place of someone with a visual handicap:

"To the blind, all things are sudden." Test this yourself: move about all the room with your eyes closed. All encounters become abrupt. Emptiness combines with sudden interface. Connections are lacking. The gradations, shadings and continuities of the visual world are gone. [...] Contemporary fashion is full of hard-edge design The experience it evokes is not visual: it is tactile.[8]

Afflicted by a grave form of myopia, Irene Brin had always been familiar with that state. In "Occhi socchiusi"[9] ("Eyes Half Shut"), one of her first articles, published in the Genoese newspaper *Il Lavoro* way back in 1933, she had felt the need not only to describe the sensory experience of the shortsighted person through the fictional character of Giorgiana, but above all to reflect on the cogent connection between the phenomenology of perception and the world of appearances. And now, more than thirty years after she had written that article, the thoughts of that singular philosopher of the media, who had made a theory out of what she had personally experienced with sensitivity and a touch of eccentricity every since the beginning of her journalistic career, must have been disturbing if not illuminating. The character of Giorgiana in "Occhi socchiusi" ("Eyes Half Shut") embodied in advance what McLuhan was to identify as the condition of perception created by fashion at the end of the sixties: that of "a world where the eye listens, the ear sees, and all the senses assist each other in concert, in a many-layered symphony of all the senses."[10] Giorgiana experienced the tactile, three-dimensional quality of clothing, a genuine "extension of the skin,"[11] a prosthetic device between her body and its surroundings:

You cannot know, people-who-see-well, how important for her are the voices, the movements, the neckties of her friends, and the gratitude she feels to those who, by faithfully wearing a red hat or a pale tobacco-colored jacket or being of gigantic height or having their hair dyed platinum blond, allow her to recognize them at once. Extremely elegant women, on the other hand, and normal men are thorns in her sociable heart; they give her, in fact, the half-shut eyes, the sorrowful expression, that make her look like Marlene.[12]


It was from Giorgiana's perspective that Irene Brin the fashion journalist began to look at clothing without prefiguring it *a priori* or anticipating its effect, but passing through it in such a way as to sense its surface, to make it vibrate in the flow of language into fragments of knowledge, capable of circulating with the other signs that say the world is in movement and that contemplate the circumstance of this.

Unlike other women journalists and writers of those years, equally engaged in commenting on fashion with passion, she did not emphasize the purely technical and sartorial aspect of clothing in her work, nor examine the modification of styles in relation to the changing lifestyles of women on the basis of an analysis that took the identity of being and appearing as a paradigm. The paradigm of the perfect transparence between the garment and the person revealing itself, in its programmatic rationality, and democratic nature, to be in fact elitist, like the one that destroys the meaning of the experience of fashion: formative precisely in so far as it is an experience of the not perfect coincidence between those two entities, and so, among broad strata of the public, a means of access to the construction of a satisfactory self-image. When in 1945, in the second edition of *Bellezza*, Irene Brin would begin to focus her articles on the subject of fashion, she would choose just this play of coincidences and mismatches between the clothing and the person as the preferred ground of her reflection. And this would be a sign of the maturity, including the stylistic maturity, attained by her "discourse" on fashion.


MORELLA

Ever since the articles of the thirties, which did not fall within the specific field of militant fashion journalism, Irene Brin's writing had been polarized around a personage, often female, a sort of figurative filter that would prove to be a congenial instrument for reporting on the creation of fashion. This character – different every time but always credible, whether drawn from reality or the fruit of invention, and barely suggested through the play of words – was brought into focus in contiguity with the clothing. So the garment, or rather the outfit, was brought to life in Irene Brin's writing all of a piece with the figure that wore it. Emblematic in this sense is the pioneering portrait that she presented of Morella:

Her friends suddenly realize that they don't know Morella at all, except what they can grasp by comparing the different images they have of her. They don't know if she is big or small, sturdy or slender, ugly or very beautiful. The person who saw her on the balcony yesterday declares that she is striking and attractive; the ones who play golf with her find her small and muscular. Have you seen her in a beret? She looks very ugly, but if she knots that rainbow scarf around her neck...
Oh, what is Morella like? They know all about her, her clothes, her house, her thoughts, her cocktail recipes: but not her. [...]
Sometimes, when she's standing in front of us, we feel we can capture her for a while, in her truth of the moment. Here she is, at the bar of the Tennis Club, in a straight white dress, low-heeled shoes, a few freckles on her nose, the calm expression of a German girl. Morella, immobile, immutable: we can say we know her, we have caught her.
But it's not true. Because all she has to do is run toward the court, and her skirt splits in two, revealing a pair of loose sports pants. They turn her run into the ambiguous dance of a handsome pageboy, lend her a mysterious and loose lightness. She knows it, and is happy about it. She turns around, as if to laugh at us.[13]

Couched in a language of representation that appropriates the modes of photography, the figure of Morella, frozen in a succession of poses, passes from style to style, from posture to posture: in her multiple performances she is not tied to a psychological need, nor to a precise physiognomy of identity that would give her the stimulus needed to enter a fully narrative dimension. A creature who is all surface, Morella offers those who look at her a zone of "optical resistance," and one that exacts a toll of suffering. We are tempted to go beyond her appearance, to undermine her stubbornly self-referential character and invest her with the feelings and the imagination of we who are looking at her. By limiting herself to her appearance, Morella draws the reader's gaze to her body, welded to her clothing, to her gestures rendered more or less free and easy by the consistency of the fabrics,

by the inevitability of the cut. And even the attempt at a barely
hinted voyeurism is fated to shatter against the shock wave of the
writer's subtle and pungent irony:

We meet her, dressed in black, with a little hat pulled down over her eye, and she
looks like a Parisian girl of 1903, terribly snobbish. She will take off her jacket, to
show us her black and white blouse, its sleeves puffed with organdie, and a cravat
ready to fly away. The organdie suggests to her, in fact, a series of stylized
movements and whims that make her look unreal, like a teenager in an English
novel. But, as soon as she can, she'll take off the skirt as well, giving us a fright. But
we're wrong: we see the extension of the blouse: this white dress, printed in black,
the same as ours: it is today's Morella. How long will she last?
[...] Morella hesitates, between the styles and faces that she puts on and takes off
every day: she likes them all, and none of them. She looks in her mirror, which
doesn't know her yet, like her friends, like herself. With eyes half shut she gazes at
the phantoms of all the Morellas that are her, but not completely. She sighs: Oh, I'd
like to find my hat, and myself. I'd like to be true to myself.[14]

"With eyes half shut," Morella shifts, confines the gaze to her own
clothed and situated corporeality, in its quality of an "always open
construction of material identity, as worldly dimension of
subjectivity."[15] Presented in these terms for the consumption of the
world, the character is already moving in the orbit of fashion: she
foreshadows the role of the model by becoming a pure unfolding, if
not a breeding ground, of modes of conduct, "attitudes," lifestyles.
And yet she is shrouded in a veil of "melancholic frenzy"[16]: in her
frantic transformation from style to style she is driven to betray the
promise to be true to herself. The externalization of her inner being
in the performative and seductive play of appearances brings a sense
of loss: Irene Brin's writing reflected it in the terms of a change of
her own modes of representation, which tended more and more
towards a "superficial" and immediate portrayal of experience.

WRITING AND TAKING PHOTOGRAPHS
In the thirties Irene Brin tried to develop a light and flexible
approach to reporting on usage and custom: a way of writing that she
would find helpful in delineating the mutable and multifaceted
profile of the generation that grew up between the wars, as she was to

present it in her book *Usi e Costumi 1920-1940*.[17] The aim of the
publication was not, and nor could it have been, not even transversely
(as she made clear in the introduction to the book), the history of a
couple of decades, "but only an aid to understanding a noisy,
ingenuous and sad generation, that deluded itself that it was living at
an exceptional pace."[18]From the perspective adopted by Irene Brin,
remote from the monumental and epic tone of the regime, the story
of this generation became the discontinuous and fragmented account
of a way of life made up of minor, ephemeral, marginal acts.
Gestures, poses, manias, little curiosities; desires, frustrations,
pleasures: the whole variegated gamut of emotions and attitudes,
accretions of the daily conduct of the emerging mass society, was
identified and conveyed notwithstanding the vulgarity, and the
indifference, of the ruling powers. It was on the tricky terrain of
fashion, fads and manners that the rapid, incisive and precise writing
of Irene Brin brought into focus fragments of individual existences,
salvaged for a moment from the inexorable flow of time in the way
that only the photographic flash can do.

They say that in the immediate postwar period the camera was the catalyst for casual
acquaintances: "Miss, may I take your picture?" asked the war veterans, now dressed
in very short jackets, and gleaming leggings. And it seems that the request could get
you a long way. It's frightening now to think of the tons of film that in those twenty
years captured endless faces, streets, beaches, stiff-lipped smiles galore, clouds
rimmed with light, pant creases, children, dogs, cats, old ladies, fishermen, groups of
horrible bathers, etc., etc., the dross of a new vice. The advent of the Leica and the
Contax increased the flood of pictures, by raising the number of photographs that an
amateur could take with a single roll from eight to thirty-six.[19]

Perhaps it was only through the mechanical eye of the photographic
lens that it had been possible to begin to reconstruct without too
much pain the relationships between people, and the new relations
between them and the objects in the social panorama, as it appeared
at that time, ravaged and wounded by the devastation of the war.
Photography, a sort of inventory of reality, an atomized reality,
represented instant by instant as if it could no longer be contained
within the perspective of an overall view, opened up to the languages
of positions and gestures, individual and collective, endlessly

reproducible, in images that no longer had the any need for the mediation of the syntactic procedures of the pen and pencil. This technological recording of experience did not require any particular know-how. It became a tool that everyone could use, a genuine means of mass communication that profoundly and thoroughly altered the mode of sensorial and intellectual comprehension of reality.

The passage on photography betrays a dismay that we can translate tentatively into the following questions: what effect has the inordinate growth of visual culture had on the processes and models of verbal and literary representation? What challenge do the endless faces, the clouds edged with light, the creases in pants that tons of rolls of film have showered us with over the course of time present to the writer?

They are complicated questions, but ones that we have no intention here to examine from the viewpoint of the theoretical debate over the relationship and the competition between the arts that has raged in modern culture since the time of Lessing's *Laocoön*. Rather it is from a somewhat eccentric perspective, distinctly permeated by the languages of contemporaneity, such as that of fashion as it is represented by Irene Brin, that this analysis starts out.

In fact the exteriorized personality of Morella is represented as if Irene Brin were disposed to share the modality of a visual system that works without the complex mediation of the memory, something that is on the other hand essential between vision and the hand in the technique of drawing.[20] An art that can in fact be practiced even *in absentia* of an actual referent. Conversely, the photograph, as a photochemical trace, i.e. the mark made by light on a photosensitive surface that captures its impression, absolutely requires, as a necessary condition, the presence of a material referent. The reference "is the founding order of Photography,"[21] and yet that actuality is conveyed to us literally as a phantom by the camera: "with eyes half shut" Morella "gazes at the phantoms of all the Morellas that are her, but not completely."[22] The photographic or pseudo-photographic image lives on the ambivalence of being at one and the same time an *analogon* of the real thing and its ghostly representation. Life is conveyed in the image through "a micro-version of death."[23] A rapid and decided movement of the hand doing the bidding of the eye looking through the lens[24] exorcizes the fear of death. In a fraction of

a second the photograph places life and death under the shadow of
ephemeral fruition, of which its very perishability is a tangible sign.
The shot frees us from the exemplifying and perpetual power of
memory, both as souvenir and as monument.
In his 1927 essay "Photography," Kracauer wrote:

Photography grasps what is given as a spatial (or temporal) continuum; memory
images retain what is given only insofar as it has significance. Since what is
significant is not reducible to either merely spatial or merely temporal terms,
memory images are at odds with photographic representation. From the latter's
perspective, memory images appear to be fragments – but only because photography
does not encompass the meaning to which they refer and in relation to which they
cease to be fragments. Similarly, from the perspective of memory, photography
appears as a jumble that consists partly of garbage.[25]

From those tons of film that have invaded the world, becoming "the
comprehensive catalogue of all manifestations which present
themselves in space,"[26] life has gradually withdrawn, taking with it
the awareness of that datum of reality that the photo reproduces. This
is why Irene Brin the writer is filled with dismay: the photograph
reveals its indifference to the meaning of what it portrays and the
compulsion to take pictures – what used to be called a "vice" in the
past – produces "dross": i.e. the flood of photos that "sweeps away the
dams of memory"[27] and swallows up a world that seems almost to
aspire to turn into a spatial continuum, into pure surface. There is
nothing left but to linger over the external features of what is
represented and from this frontier embark on a remodeling of the
gaze increasingly spellbound by the details of fashion: "It is the
fashion details that hold the gaze tight. Photography is bound to
time in precisely the same way as fashion."[28]
Both, photography and fashion, lead naturally to the world of daily
newspapers, of illustrated magazines: i.e. to the medium that Irene
Brin chose as her field of expression.

"IRENE BRIN"
She had been unable to resist the allure of printed paper ever since
the time when, at a very early age, a newspaper in Genoa had

proposed that she cover "run-over dogs," an expression that was used at the time to define the society piece: "None of the editors wanted to cover run-over dogs, metaphorically or not, except this young, shortsighted girl with long legs and an insatiable curiosity."[29]
She was an attentive and precise observer of daily life in the early thirties, one who described with tact, but also with subtle irony, the styles of life embodied in the figures she came across in the haunts of elegant society in the lively provincial capital of Liguria, as well as in more domestic surroundings, where the gestures of routine were never banal, never reduced to stereotyped figures.
The critical appreciation of this writing can never be disconnected from the awareness that it was created for the medium of journalism, whose specific qualities intimately pervade even her works of narrative, to the point that every venture into the autonomous form of the book was shaped and presented by the writer in the manner of the original journalistic model.
Looking at the list of contents of *Usi e Costumi 1920-1940*, what we find are titles of the various columns that make up the structure of newspapers and periodicals: "Whims and Charms," "High Society," "Celebrities," "Travel," "Home Furnishing," "The Kitchen", ending with a long series of "Miscellaneous Events," taken to the letter from reports in the national and international press. This tendency was to recur over time, although with different nuances according to the circumstances, as if in a sort of compulsive repetition. And if *Usi e Costumi 1920-1940* was the first manifestation of this in order of time, I would like to take a leap forward here and close the circle, by going straight to her last narrative work. This is a long fragment of an autobiographical character, as yet unpublished, that dates, like the article on "revealing a genius," from 1968, the year before her death. *1952, L'Italia che esplode* ("1952, Exploding Italy"),[30] is the title of this curious work, in which autobiography is mixed up with the historical, cultural and social events of a year in the country's life. That year is 1952: the date of the official investiture of Italian fashion in the institutional Sala Bianca of Palazzo Pitti. The work was to have been included in the series "365... a Year in the Life of..." edited by Milena Milani for Immordino Editore of Genoa.

The title of the series says it all. This book is the story of a year. Personally, the year that marked a turning point in my already fairly long life, a life that has been no more and no less dramatic than that of other Italians. Nationally, it was the year that saw Italy, barely healed and as poor as ever, explode out of its confines in an atmosphere of intelligent and tatterdemalion celebration.[31]

In this story the titles of the chapters, one for each of the twelve months of the solar year, do not escape the compositional logic of the newspaper or the magazine. We get the impression we are looking at a series of features: "The Photographers, the Photographed, the Bash for Carmel Snow," " The Visconti, the Suitcases, the Flights," "The Great Summer of the Cinema," "Cultural Exchanges and the Discovery of America," "Laudomia del Drago, the Bride of the Year, the New Booms were Three: Theaters, Renovated Apartments and above All Extemporary Poetry," "The Society of Dolts, the Importance of Translations, Orgies of Magic and Cats in the Window." It really is the "dross of a new vice" – the vice of taking photographs, with or without the camera – that emerges through these snapshots. Perhaps the strangest of all is the title that introduces the Irene Brin "personality": "Irenebrinentrano, Irenebrindano, Irenebrinescono." A series of untranslatable plays on words that transform her name into a verb, this curious formula is in reality a citation of an editorial published between 1938 and 1939 by the satirical journal *Bertoldo*, precocious in its perception of the presence of a fashionable phenomenon: that of the writer and journalist "Irene Brin." A name that was in reality the pseudonym of the writer and journalist Maria Vittoria Rossi. It had been created for her, with affection, by Leo Longanesi:

I am not called either Irene, or Brin, even if that's how I appear in contracts, telephone directories and family discussions. They are names invented by Leo Longanesi. I am an invention of Leo Longanesi, like many other people who have been lucky enough to pass him by, to stir in some way his interest, to rouse his furious constructive patience.[32]

That invention brought her luck. However, the writer had had an unsettled account with her name for some years already. She had published her first piece anonymously in the newspaper *Il Lavoro*. Later, she had signed the articles she was writing with different pseudonyms, colored by the circumstances: first it was "Marlene," then "Oriane," "Marina Turr" and "Geraldina Tron." As "Adelina" she signed accounts of a housewife's life, and then, without a break, there were "Madame d'O," "Morella," "Ortensia" and many others. She became "Contessa Clara" for the readers' letters and "Cécil Aldighieri" for the television reviews. Other articles bore the signature 'mariù', a diminutive by which the writer was known in her family, or "Mariù Rossi." From 1937, the year of her marriage, she added to her first name the surname of her husband Gaspero del Corso.

So it was a long series of names that she scattered over the pages of newspapers and magazines, with the nonchalance of a change of clothing, during thirty-seven years of brisk and enthusiastic work. The reader was faced with a real proliferation of pseudonyms, perhaps not fully appreciated at the time. And yet, looked back on from a distance, the curious series of *noms de plume* does not jar: rather, it invites us to enter into a sort of fictional convention. We can imagine that in many articles on fashion the signature "Madame d'O" had been influenced by the evocative pseudonyms with which Mallarmé signed his articles in *La Dernière Mode*, a genuine masterpiece of the inability to distinguish between the real and the fictional:

There is no subject more delicate, more dangerous, more bitter. Futile for contemporaries, it would become mysterious for posterity, and anyone who reads today the chronicles of Miss Satin or Marguerite de Ponty in the magazine yellowing or crackling with decrepitude that was entitled *Dernière Mode* would find it difficult to recognize fashion in the *Dernière Mode* and a single poet in its two charming ladies: Stéphane Mallarmé. Mallarmé adored his little women's magazine, and was not just its editor in chief, but responsible for almost everything, hiding behind twenty different pseudonyms, which included a Creole cook and a horticulturist from Nice. However, his favorite was Miss Satin, with her sibilant and lustrous name [...].[33]

## PRECIOUS MIMICRY

In many articles the choice of pseudonym tended to abolish any distance between the writer and the reader, nurturing inter-individual processes of projection and imaginary identification in which we can recognize the social dynamics of the emerging Italian cultural industry, singled out by Irene Brin with extreme accuracy.

In the article "Pianto per Jean" ("Lament for Jean") of 1937, signed "mariù" and dedicated to the American actress Jean Harlow, the superposition of author/reader/personality reflects the sentimental correspondence, the reciprocal consumption of image and imagination between the Hollywood star and the type of "Today's girl":

Many women have mourned the death of Miss Harlow: humble, rather bashful tears; but you can't think about her dead without grieving: she was so beautiful, radiant. Many women have mourned themselves, since there was in Jean Harlow [a] precious mimicry that led her to play the role of Today's girl, resembling innumerable girls, who at once dreamed of being like her. This warm current of understanding gave her greater humanity, and greater charm to the others. After all our manicurist, when she tosses her curls and smiles at you sideways, looks like Jean; but Jean, when she burst into bitter sobs and gentle fits of anger, went straight to the heart of our manicurist.[34]

This play of mirrors, that we can think of as a sort of *mise en abîme* of the personage, answers to a logic of interaction between the world of the screen and the world of reality: the screen becomes the catalyst of the self-perception of individuals, who, however, explain themselves in a narration that presents not so much people as "figures," superficial natures, natures that can be reproduced on either side of the screen. It is no accident that the expression "precious mimicry" is used in the article, words that may remind us of the reflections in the essay "Mimétisme et psychasténie légendaire" written by Roger Caillois in 1935 for the magazine *Minotaure*. Caillois analyzes the phenomenon of mimicry in the praying mantis, surrealistically inventing an interdisciplinary field somewhere between entomology and a sort of psychobiology – if we can call it that – where human beings and insects share the same kind of behavior. Caillois does not connect mimicry in the insect with a means of adaptation for defensive purposes or to ensure survival, but ascribes it a function operating exclusively in the visual sphere: thus he associates the phenomenon with the perception that the insect itself has of its spatial surroundings. In this context Caillois proposes an interpretation of mimicry as a kind of psychosis on the insect's part: a loss of the capacity to distinguish itself, to maintain a difference from the environment in which it is immersed. So the insect yields to a 'confusion' with what surrounds it. From this point of view, the figure no longer answers to a logic of identity: it is perceived as the result of a process of erosion of subjectivity, of an unchecked practice of "exfoliation," which gives rise to a whole colony of presences. What emerges is the fascination of not belonging to oneself, of abdication from the self, of sinking into the flow of images, caught in their turn in the incandescence of the magnesium flash.[35]

With the consolidation of the fictional nature of the personality even the figure of the writer is modified: the authorial tone is weakened, while the journalistic one tends to prevail. The "mosaic" technology typical of the press page is studied in such a way as to bring together and give form to that plurality of information that conveys to us "the inside story of the community in action and interaction"[36] It does not favor a detached point of view, as the "book" form does: "it entails the disappearance of the author,"[37] his or her reduction to a small figure in the background of an "impersonal art of juxtaposition as revolutionary and democratic also in the sense that it enables each reader to be an artist."[38] So the daily and periodical press work as a space in which writing and reading coexist as reciprocal and simultaneous phenomena. This digression in which names, pseudonyms and writing are interwoven and hybridized in favor of the only aspiration representable, which is that of the personality, can only be brought to an end by returning to the formula from *Bertoldo* that opens *1952, L'Italia che esplode*: "Irenebrinentrano, Irenebrindano, Irenebrinescono." The bizarre linguistic invention, permeated by a vein of humor and parody directed at the Irene Brin phenomenon both for her precocious and unusual presence in the press of the time and for the power of seduction she exercised over so many of her contemporaries – from schoolgirls to established writers, "all intent on coming out every week with imitation Irene Brin articles and lifestyles?"[39]– becomes the emblem of a coming and going between many characters. I think she chose that formula to open her autobiographical account not just because it conveyed a precise cultural and social climate in a lively way, but also because it summed up the cultural construction of a subjectivity that was conceived as singular-plural: whose consistency was wholly contingent, modeled and woven on the surface. The different presences that little by little emerged and took shape formed part of an out-and-out practice of transfiguration based entirely on manipulation of the codes of appearance. In accordance with the aesthetics of camp,[40] the personage was no longer brought into visibility along a route that delineates its development. It did not let itself be followed along the lines of a *Bildung* that dissected its psychological traits, structured according to a coherence and integrity of gaze that aimed at the completeness of a portrait, however imaginary. There was no longer, in fact, a unitary and univocal consciousness inside or outside the personage, which was now on the contrary shaped by sections through an operation of 'treatment' and assembly, that grasped it from the outside, in the serial play of appearances: in the flagrancy of a gesture, an expression, a dialogue. The presences evoked now inhabited a media landscape – be it clothing or cinema screen – and were ready to be consumed or to be trained to consume themselves.

It is for this reason that shaping them entailed a form of writing that ever more closely resembled the equipment used for technical reproduction. An almost photographic flash that solarized them or blew them up to the point of making them crumble away or reducing them to a black hole, contracting them until they imploded. It was a mode of representation that presented not so much "figures," or ways of being, as a fantasy of "rewriting" themselves and the world. The writer identified rewriting – she used the English term in the article "Un nome inventato" ("An Invented Name"), dedicated to Leo Longanesi – as the matrix of a continual and unstoppable process of stylization of the person, rendered flexible through effects of fluid identity inscribed in the material datum of the writing.

There is a verb in English that has recently become popular in other languages too, "to rewrite," which the French turn into *revriter*, and which has taken on a legal standing. [...] Longanesi *rewrote* not just our writings, but our brains.[41]

A practice, that of "rewriting," which allowed her, in a gesture of self-mockery, to adopt the parodic formula of *Bertoldo* at the beginning of the account of her life and work, conscious that there was no original to imitate, so that the parody was in effect aimed at this very notion. Instead, on each occasion, it would be possible to proceed with the rewriting of what was given as the initial referent, in the awareness that what was produced, produced in its turn a marginality that could no longer be metabolized.

As a mark of her well-deserved celebrity, many photographs of Irene Brin can be found in the press. None of them resembles any of the others, but all look like the original, as she was at the moment the picture was taken. There is a blonde Irene Brin, as diaphanous and transparent as a sheath of cellophane, and there is another, dark-haired one, as solid and nocturnal as a crow's wing. There is one in the classical style, as plump and full as a quail; and there is a Gothic one, as slender and twisted as a snake. The blonde Irene talks, dresses and even thinks in a very different way from the brunette Irene; the plump Irene moves, does her hair and even writes in a very different way from the slender one. How the hell she manages, this woman, to put on weight and lose it in the space of a few hours, only she knows, or perhaps even she doesn't know.[42]

This is what Indro Montanelli wrote in 1952, in a portrait of Irene Brin, his close friend and esteemed colleague, grasping perhaps the most disconcerting trait of her personality, the one that inevitably links her to the nature of her own personage: Morella.

"How do I look?" she asks me all of a sudden, and I'm left speechless for a moment, accustomed as I am to Irene's coquetry when it is covert, but not when it is overt: "Great!" I answer, with absolute sincerity. "A rose in bloom!" Mariù shakes her head at that platitude, smiles, squeezes my arm. "Gallantry is not your forte, my dear Indro, and that's not what I meant. I wanted to know if my face, if you think that at last it has attained a definitive expression..." And she scrutinized me anxiously through her lorgnette. "Dear Mariù, your face has always had a definitive expression. It's just that the definitions keep changing."[43]

NOTE_____

[1] Irene Brin, "Rivelare un genio sì, un amore segreto no," in *Harper's Bazaar Italia*, no. 1, 1969, p. 3.
[2] *Ibid.*
[3] *Ibid.*
[4] *Ibid.*
[5] *Ibid.*
[6] Marshall McLuhan, *Understanding Media: The Extensions of Man*. New York: New American Library, 1964; repr. Cambridge, (MA): MIT Press, 1994.
[7] Marshall McLuhan, "Fashion è medium," in Paola Colaiacomo, Vittoria C. Caratozzolo (eds.), *Mercanti di stile*. Rome: Editori Riuniti, 2002, p. 207.
[8] Ivi, pp. 211-12.
[9] Irene Brin, "Occhi socchiusi," in *Il Lavoro*, October 25, 1933.
[10] Marshall McLuhan, "Fashion è medium," in P. Colaiacomo, V.C. Caratozzolo (eds.), *Mercanti di stile*, cit., p. 212.

[11] Marshall McLuhan, *The Medium is the Massage*. New York: Simon & Schuster, 1967, p. 26.

[12] Irene Brin, "Occhi socchiusi," cit.

[13] Irene Brin, "Fedeltà di Morella," in *Il Lavoro*, April 23, 1933.

[14] *Ibid.*

[15] Patrizia Calefato, *Mass moda. Linguaggio e immaginario del corpo rivestito*. Genoa: Costa & Nolan, 1996, p. 8.

[16] Irene Brin, *Usi e Costumi 1920-1940*. Rome: Donatello De Luigi, 1944, p. 111.

[17] Irene Brin, *Usi e Costumi 1920-1940*, cit.

[18] *Ibid.*

[19] Ivi, pp. 39-40.

[20] Cf. Paul Valéry, *Degas Dance Drawing*. New York: Lear, 1948.

[21] Roland Barthes, *Camera Lucida. Reflections on Photography*, New York: Hill and Wang, 1982, p. 77.

[22] Irene Brin, "Fedeltà di Morella," cit.

[23] R. Barthes, *Camera Lucida. Reflections on Photography*, cit., p. 14.

[24] Cf. Walter Benjamin, *The Work of Art in the Age of Mechanical Reproduction*. New York: Schocken Books, 1968.

[25] Siegfried Kracauer, "Photography," in Id., *The Mass Ornament: Weimar Essays* (*Ornament der Masse*, 1927), trans. by Thomas Y. Levin. Cambridge (MA): Harvard University Press, 1995, pp. 50-1.

[26] *Ibid.*

[27] *Ibid.*

[28] Ivi, p. 55.

[29] Irene Brin, *1952, L'Italia che esplode*, [unpublished], quoted from the typescript, p. 5.

[30] The autobiographical account was never published by Immordino Editore. At the moment a typewritten copy of the text is preserved in the Fondo L'Obelisco in the Historical Archives of the Galleria Nazionale d'Arte Moderna. A different and perhaps earlier version than the one at the GNAM exists in incomplete form in the Irene Brin Archives, kept at the cultural association La Centrale dell'Arte.

[31] Irene Brin, *1952, L'Italia che esplode*, [unpublished], quoted from the typescript, p. 1.

[32] Irene Brin, "Un nome inventato," in *Il Borghese*, yr. VIII, (1957), no. 41, pp. 588-9. The issue of the magazine, devoted in its entirety to its late editor Leo Longanesi, contained articles and reminiscences by Vincenzo Cardarelli and Emilio Cecchi, Giuseppe Prezzolini and Henry Furst, Indro Montanelli and Giovanni Ansaldo, among others.

[33] Irene Brin, "Sapere raccontare," in *Il Giornale d'Italia*, October 11, 1953.

[34] Irene Brin, "Pianto per Jean," in *Il Lavoro*, June 20, 1937.

[35] Cf. Rosalind Krauss, *Teoria e storia della fotografia*. Milan: Bruno Mondadori, 1990.

[36] Marshall McLuhan, *Understanding Media: The Extensions of Man*. New York: New American Library, 1964; repr. Cambridge (MA): MIT Press, 1994, p. 205.

[37] Roland Barthes, *Le Bruissement de la langue*. Paris: Seuil, 1984; Engl. ed. "The Death of the Author," trans. by Richard Howard, in *The Rustle of Language*. New York: Hill and Wang, 1986, pp. 49-55.

[38] Marshall McLuhan, *The Interior Landscape: The Literary Criticism of Marshall McLuhan 1943-1962*, ed. by Eugene McNamara. Toronto: McGraw Hill, 1969. The quote has been translated from the Italian edition, *Il paesaggio interiore*. Milan: Sugarco, 1994, p. 36.

[39] Irene Brin, *1952, L'Italia che esplode*, [unpublished], quoted from the typescript, p. 1. The expression "with imitation Irene Brin articles and lifestyles" is a translation of the Italian word *brinate*, coined by the author to define the modes of behavior adopted by her most faithful readers in imitation of their favorite's lifestyle.

[40] Cf. Susan Sontag, "Notes on 'Camp,'" in Id., *Camp: Queer Aesthetics and the Performing Subject: A Reader*, ed. by Fabio Cleto. Ann Arbor: University of Michigan Press, 1999.

[41] Irene Brin, "Un nome inventato," in *Il Borghese*, cit.

[42] Indro Montanelli, "Irene Brin," in *Rapaci in cortile*. Milan: Longanesi, 1952, pp. 38-9.

[43] Ivi, p. 43.

Via

# I REALIZED THAT ROME WAS BECOMING THE CENTER OF THE WORLD

## BELLEZZA

Irene Brin's signature appeared in the very first issue (January 1941): "I'm proud to remember that I contributed to the first issue of *Bellezza*, at the invitation of Gio Ponti," the writer would recall years later.[1] At the time she was a war correspondent in Yugoslavia, and certainly could not devote her attention to fashion. In Rijeka, then an Italian possession and called Fiume, she had a delivery address at the Piva pastry shop.

I arrived there using strange means, by sea and by land, and rushed to Piva, where I found my mail and the proofs to correct for *Documento*, *Storia* and *Bellezza*. It was odd to strip Mrs. X of an adjective, correct the title of bride Y, while the dear salesgirls scraped together a meal for me, which I ate greedily.[2]

It was not until November 1945, when the war was over and a new series of the magazine was launched, that the journalist started to contribute to *Bellezza* again, with a series of articles in which she want back to reflecting on fashion: not exclusively in terms of the creation of new lines, but as a phenomenon of much broader scope that still had to be mapped. Her gaze, already schooled in the interpretation of custom, was now ready to investigate the link between production and consumption in its interrelations with the variegated social and cultural scene of the city. And Rome was the privileged space for this exploration, and for comparison with the never forgotten reality of Northern European and America.

### THE SUPERFLUOUS

With the new series of *Bellezza* Irene Brin's name appeared on the editing board alongside those of the two illustrators, Brunetta Mateldi and Federico Pallavicini; the new editor in chief was Michelangelo Testa and the managing editor Elsa Robiola. The nightmare of the war was finally over but, as far as fashion was concerned, there was still a strong prejudice against a field of experience dismissed as "frivolous" and "superfluous." What a "break" it must have seemed, therefore, to read the article by Gio Ponti, in the role of special contributor, in the same issue of the magazine. "È superfluo il superfluo?" ("Is the Superfluous Superfluous?") was the provocative title he chose for his article. In it he discussed the significance that should be given to the "superfluous" in a country undergoing reconstruction, that was in pursuit of a better quality of life, above the level of mere survival. His brief analysis started out from an observation of the urban fabric, the most favorable to the revival of relations between individuals. The point of view he assumed was that of a "city-trotter," wandering through the streets of a Milan cruelly scarred by war but already set to demonstrate its vitality, its yearning for new modes of existence:

This vitality of the superfluous, which is reemerging so victoriously, irrepressibly and movingly from the ruins, is a great sign for the future of us Italians, of how alive in us is the need for loveliness, for a touch of beauty, a deeply civilized need for something that goes beyond the pure and simple fact of existing. [...] It has always been with deep emotion that our roaming observer has noticed, even in terrible times, the presence in our beloved women of a care for their personal appearance, of an elegance, of an upbringing that bears witness to their awareness of another delicate and indispensable thing, to be saved along with the rest from the tragic wreck. And this thing, their charm, has been symbolically saved. Indeed, our wanderer around Italy notes that the disappearance of heavy thick-soled shoes and their replacement by light sandals, and the greater attractiveness of some hairstyles and the other odd, restrained touch of care for the person are the marks of a superior elegance, of a refinement already attained.[3]

It was precisely this appreciation of the temporary and the superfluous, so audaciously put forward by Gio Ponti, that animated Irene Brin's writings on fashion: her way of looking so carefully at new forms of existence, her personas and characters who experimented with unprecedented approaches to an everyday life characterized by styles that were being adapted to the contingency of the world. Gradually, her discourse on fashion was stripped of its high-flown manner, becoming all-encompassing: it was conveyed through snapshots and phrases stolen from the muddled and erratic conversations overhead in fashionable haunts.

In the first article she wrote for the new series of *Bellezza*, entitled "Il Nord e il Sud," ("The North and the South") she compared events drawn from the news reports of those days with images evoking stills from newsreels, immediately bestowing on the writing the character of a medium hybridized with other forms of communication.

At the center of the analysis, the woman of the North and the woman of the South: the shadow of the war and the regime still lies on their clothes, on their shoes, on their gestures, on their words; but equally evident is the enthusiasm and curiosity that the two women show in observing each other; in creatively learning the lesson of the foreign magazines, now accessible again; in exchanging information about what they're wearing, about how it should be interpreted. In short the country, from South to North and back again, can also be reunified in the name of frivolity: with the dissemination of a new accessory, of a novel cut of dress, of a precious sandal, of an earring made by the designer Luciana. But unifying too is the awareness of the existence of a "faraway," of ways of living in the world that allow a new shaping of the persona, an unexpected performativity. What emerges is the communicative nature of fashion, the way it originates in a local specificity, its propensity to cross over, to hybridize with the most disparate uses and customs, to be a currency that can be spent anywhere. And the accessories, which glitter to our eyes even if only as a consequence of her special ability to convey all of their magic, are assimilated to the figure, assembled into a new entity: the fashionable personality.

The article opens with the image of another North and South, those of the epic *Gone with the Wind*. It is just a brief allusion, and yet one that is highly effective in the way it suggests an emotional wavelength that has an influence, through crossover from the experience of the movie make-believe, on the circumstances that affect the personages of this cross-section of the fashion world.

Repudiating any evocation of crinolines and flounces offered by the North and South of *Gone with the Wind*, our South in flat shoes and our North in cork soles confront one another over pontoon bridges and roads strewn with rubble. A modest but easygoing South, a modest but proud North, and the women who have just got down from trucks covered with dust represent two kinds of fashion independent to the point of separatism, something corroborated by the testimonies of the American fashion magazine that has come to Rome and the French fashion magazine that has come to Turin. [...] There are infiltrations, which take on the appearance of treachery: a girl from Milan, after careful study of a New York magazine, adopts the single shoulder strap for her swimming costume and introduces it in Rapallo; a Neapolitan passing through Santa Margherita discovers wraps of white Angora wool and the short dress of white lace with a crimson and fuchsia belt and decks herself out in them at home. Golden sandals, held in place by a star which sets between first and second toe not just an elaborate means of securing their steps, but also an undoubted symbol of sea and sky, are spreading from Via Condotti to Via Montenapoleone, crossing paths with tall umbrellas [...] widened by a flounce around the crown, perfect for the sun and yet totally waterproof and ready to invade Rome. Little stratagems of poor but graceful people, inventions for courageous women, but marred by regret: "I'm twenty-two," sighs Elisabetta, "a husband, two children and I've still never worn a gown, I've never been to a real ball!" And Cristina: "I'm thirty-one and have to adopt the motto of my grandmother when she was seventy, *à notre âge, mon enfant on ne s'habille pas, on se couvre!*" And each sincerely hopes that from regions still hard to reach, mysterious when reckoned in terms of kilometers and punctured tires, will come at least the possibility of an exchange: who will place in Harry's Bar in Venice the memorial plaque (in printed silk) recording an almost historic encounter, a Vanity Fair transformed to the point of being moving? They didn't know each other at all. The woman of the South stood in front of the counter in a dress of highly synthetic jersey, already darned in the furrows of its drapery; the woman of the North was in the far corner, in a dress with a flower pattern that had turned into a sack after many metamorphoses: the setting moreover seemed unchanged, the not-so-young men who derived their elegance from a yellow scarf and from an air of stolidity conversing with Cipriani, the not-so-young women who relied for their seductiveness on the flawed feature, on the malignant tic which once made them suffer and which they now use as a weapon, perfecting the majesty of the nose, the wrinkling of the brow, chattering incessantly and with false interest with young men. In short the atmosphere was the same as always, an aquarium over whose glass walls the years had passed in vain and in which the wars were now represented solely and mildly by the darns in the synthetic jersey, by the alterations to the floral crêpe. And naturally it was the two postwar heroines who showed a lasting enthusiasm for frivolity when the northerner got up, ran up to the southerner and, almost breathless, asked her the secret of her earrings, took them off her and tried them on, going back proudly to the table where her friends were waiting for her, to be adorned one by one with the unexpected jewel.[4]

No banality or sense of the superfluous touches the beauty of these young women, who after the privations of the war approach the glitter of fashion with the candor and curiosity of someone about to experience the mutability of their own appearance. It is not so much the desire to possess fashionable objects that drives these so enthusiastic figures as the possibility of undergoing, through the new articles of clothing, the effects of a creative activity that works on the personal appearance: "The piece of jewellery is a *next-to-nothing*, but out of this *next-to-nothing* comes great energy."[5] Irene Brin had been able to experience the magic that the piece of jewellery works on clothing during the war, when the presence of such an ornament on faded garments, remodeled several times, made it possible to see past the poverty, the pain, the insecurity of daily life.

Who could have saved the skirts and jackets, fatefully made out of her husband's castoff coats, if she had not been able to pin onto the lapel a golden sun, rightly immense and echoed by the other one docile around her wrist? The world was gray, the curfew started at five o'clock, but from the lobe of her left ear hung a green drop, from the right a red drop, and don't ask us the reason for this whim.[6]

But that same magic is shortly to cast its spell on opulent America, as the conclusion of the article does not fail to point out, not without a touch of irony:

Arrows, bows, quivers, wings, sphinxes, hands, birds, lions, obelisks, flowers, fruit, mermaids, gentle in the curves of their gilded metal, sparkling with bits of polished glass, offer us the possibilities of a Thousand and One Nights and now, crossing the sea, will offer them to American women, unaware of the climate of perseverance and difficulty to which Luciana's discoveries probably owe their greatest charm [...].[7]

The desire of Italian women to rediscover the pleasure of carrying out an operation of self-fashioning is dialectically contrasted with the lifestyle of American women, accustomed to a very different standard of living. But the idea that the world might set off on its new course from Rome of all places did not reflect a personal conviction of Irene Brin's. In fact it was at just that time that a climate of suspense, like that of a hiatus between two eras, was created in which it seemed that Rome could become the *caput mundi* again. A period of history on which *La Dolce Vita* would set the seal with all the tenderness of a dirge. But in the summer of 1944, when the *Vogue* journalist Bettina Ballard[8] arrived in the Italian capital from North Africa, where she had been working as a volunteer for the Red Cross, the city enchanted her with its festive air. What struck her, in a city still far away from the atmosphere *à la mode* that she herself was to find when she returned there as fashion editor of *Vogue* for the shows of the early fifties, were the Roman women. Suntanned, in their freshly made clothes in bright colors, they again thronged the streets of the great city. One detail assumed an almost fetishistic significance in her eyes: almost all of them wore sandals that, in their seductive essentiality, enhanced the elegant and slender line of the foot.

The novel style of the women of Rome dispelled in an instant the glamour of the few items of clothing that Ballard had carried with her from the start of her journey. It's true that the journalist was coming from Africa and not from the salons of Paris, it's true that the frivolous and effervescent atmosphere of society life in the Roman palaces cloaked everything in splendor, but were those circumstances sufficient to make her feel unfashionable and decide to immediately fall into line with "Roman standards of fashion"[9] Certainly the circumstances played a part. In a spirit of solidarity with the shortage of clothing at that moment, Ballard had herself a dress made that was undoubtedly very different from what she was used to on the other side of the Atlantic. As she recounts in her autobiography, she got hold of the silk of a parachute from a soldier, had it dyed in the lively shades of Italian fabrics and then took it to a small dressmaker's shop – they had only just begun to reopen their doors – where the material made for war was turned into a dress.

It was an operation of a markedly artisan character that saw the

American journalist tackling a situation much closer to do-it-yourself dressmaking than to fashion proper. One cannot help but be reminded of the clothes that Simonetta Visconti had made, in that time of scarcity, out of dishtowels and gardening smocks.

Bettina Ballard at once fell into line with the pioneering spirit of the early Roman collections. However, it is still hard to understand what she really meant by the expression "Roman standards of fashion." Might it not have been her own perspective as a refined and perceptive journalist that created it, this standard? And brought it into being at the very moment she named it, thereby enrolling the elegance of Roman women in the system of fashion? Enthusiastic about the lifestyle she had encountered, she sensed that the right place for the pictures her eyes were taking of the world around her was the pages of *Vogue*. And so she put back on the shoes, castoff some time ago, of the reporter for Condé Nast's authoritative magazine: and it was by this act that the making of that adventurous Roman dress was transformed fully into "fashion."

Almost compulsively her camera lens focused on the elegant lines of the feet of Princess Galitzine who, not unlike the marble maidens of ancient Rome – a sort of second Gradiva – wore very flimsy footwear with grace: once published in *Vogue* those sandals were to literally drive thousands of American women crazy; they became the "fashion" on both sides of the ocean.

SHOP WINDOWS

The summer of 1946 arrived and Rome was already the tried-and-tested set for a varied series of narratives that directly concerned the body of the city: both the war-torn one shown by neo-realist cinema – *Roma città aperta* had come out in March 1945 – and the mythical one that was shortly to feed the voracious appetite of the Hollywood majors, about to invade Cinecittà.

There was, however, one spectacle that personally affected the crowd as it made its way through the city: that of the clothes and fashion accessories which adorned the shop windows. Objects that were used to catch the alert eye of potential buyers.

An article devoted to the phenomenology of shop windows, written by Vinicio Marinucci, had already appeared in the November 1943 issue of *Bellezza*.[10] Marinucci's analysis did not dwell on the fascination that the merchandize on display exercised on consumer-spectators. Here shop windows were not the form of urban entertainment proposed to us, classically, by Zola in his novel *The Ladies' Delight*, where the art of window dressing expressed new forms of desire and consumption. The subtle quality of this visual experience seems to have escaped Marinucci: on the other hand a custom of shopping comparable to that found elsewhere in Europe and on America was lacking in Italy. So Italian shop windows looked to the journalist like a "living museum of today's humanity."[11] They were a space that, literally, reflected the people who looked in them, presenting them with a sort of frustrating, "indirect definition of themselves." Thus any possible projection of the imagination was lost: on winter days they were not those "windows pale with mist" that could invite passersby to turn their backs on the damp and cold street and immerse themselves in the warm atmosphere of fine weather already to be found inside the store, as Zola's ladies did, feeling like they were "entering the spring [...] cooling off with the light fabrics, the flowery brilliance of the soft tints, the rustic cheer of the summer fashions and parasols."[12]

On the contrary, the shop windows described by Marinucci invited people "to escape from the unbearable loneliness of the street" in order to reach the warmth of the house as quickly as possible. This inhibited the experience, by this time rooted in the habits of the more conscious European and North American consumers, of living the space of the department store as a realm of fantasy, a mediator between the public and private sphere.[13] And so it is no coincidence that the article defined the difference between the function of the shop window and that of the mirror: while the former presented the passerby with his or her image unchanged, the mirror implied a different dimension linked directly to desire, to a virtual vision of one's own appearance that had to be censored immediately. The fear was that shop windows might disrupt our system of perception: by carrying out a sort of mild subversion of spatiotemporal coordinates in the person who paused even just for a moment in front of their fantasy.

Irene Brin sensed that exploration of the changing and multivocal quality of shop windows was relevant to her writing:

On a fierce morning in early August, a morning so dazzling with white sunlight that it almost seemed black (the sky went beyond any limit granted to deep blue, the squares were ravaged with light) Vincenza and Valentina went out for a stroll, just as if they were throwing themselves out of the window.
"Sunglasses defended them from the glare; solitude did not defend them from gloom. They were excessively free, in their already neglected sandals, in their surah dresses, which in May had seemed to them the exact expression of the necessities and decencies of summer, and, naturally without hunger, without cheer, without hope, they walked along a Via Condotti as empty as the slough of a cicada. The flight of stairs fascinated them, as a novel form of torture, and they suffered them, stair by stair, as far as a Via Sistina dazzling with hot stones. What could they hope for, in a world where their steps took them pointlessly to more scorched pavements, to more burning expenses of asphalt? It still depended on the step: appearing in the window of Frattegiani's, a sandal made of very slender strips of leather, alternating in precious shades, allowed them to hope for a walk to be taken in the cool.[14]

Fittingly, the title of the article is "Passeggiata romana,"[15] ("Roman Walk") for the motif of crossing the city is more than a simple setting in which to sketch the personalities of Vincenza and Valentina. It is the camera, or perhaps the movie camera: in any case the medium through which the writing catches them, succinctly recording their emotions and getting the reader in tune with them. There is not even the hint of a psychological sounding of the character: what we are told is all on the level of appearance, all accessible to the eye. They are exploded particles of fictional figures the ones whose *wandering* we follow, in its most ephemeral forms. The article is illustrated with sketches signed by Anna Evangelista: female figures wear models from the new collections proposed by the various ateliers, indicated at the edge of the drawings as if they were road signs, so that the writing is able to maintain its independence of the images.
Vincenza and Valentina drag themselves through the streets of the center of a sun-baked Rome at the height of summer: they move along without a goal, almost putting up a resistance to the surface they are walking on. They also resist their own feelings, absolutely contiguous with the burning asphalt: an emotional state evoked right

at the beginning of the article when we are told that the women went out with the impulsiveness of someone throwing themselves from the window. From that moment on, it is the struggle of the moving body against the fiery ground that holds together the threads of the little story, already almost a TV commercial. The pace is fast and the narrative tension cunningly held back until the moment when Vincenza and Valentina's sense of dissatisfaction and emotional drain finds immediate relief at the sight of the objects on display in the windows of the boutique. And so, once again, the appearance of a sandal is the trigger for a dream, foreshadowing cooler strolls. Until a wholly unreal seaside setting is kindled in the imagination of the two spectators by the sight of the colors and material of the summer dresses of the Gattinoni fashion house:

Now Valentina and Vicenza had grown more lively. For them the blue-and-white decor of Gattinoni's took the place of a beach, in the background of the white and light blue costume, where the large bow at the back reminded them of the bustle and the bolero closed (halfway) on golden brown shoulders. [...] Returning to the burnt heart of the old city, the friends saw truly monastic apparitions on Via Frattina, Marta Palmer putting a cowl on the little yellow dress, completed with a pocket of gold chains, no less ecclesiastical, on the cyclamen-colored crêpe of the formal robe.
Back on Via Condotti, the circle is about to close on Vicenza and Valentina, who have again found a reason to live, a faith in the possibility of joy, even if remote, even if someone else's.[16]

No longer just a scene in the background, the city is brought into the foreground, as the physical space of the atelier.

The centuries go by, the stones – and the women – do not change, identical concerns of frivolous solemnity hold Rome in delicate balance and on the second floor the deliberately gray salons accommodate an immutable clientele of princesses and an already purified, already rarefied, clientele of seductresses. [...] Before gathering enough courage to tackle the portico studded with capitals, the worn stairs of felt and the haughty and inattentive mannequins, every Nouvelle Riche has to go through a kind of novitiate that stretches from purchases of ready-to-wear garments to adventures with dressmakers-with-a-golden-touch.[17]

The symbolic parallel between the architectural quality of the atelier and the character of the clients offers a new point of view from which to look at the experience of consumption. The classicism that returns as style within the products of fashion is the climax of a sentimental as well as worldly education, to be put to the test in the practice of walking the city streets. It is understandable that a pair of sandals should attract the gaze.


OBELISCO

When, in the fall of 1946, Irene Brin decided to invest a small inheritance in setting up an art gallery with her husband Gaspero del Corso, this experience too became an opportunity for the diffusion of a new culture of fashion.

The Galleria "Obelisco", at 146 Via Sistina, was inaugurated with a major exhibition devoted to Morandi, but in the days following the private view its spaces were already being utilized for a photographic service in *Bellezza*. The worlds of art and fashion enhanced and publicized one another in the cozy rooms of the gallery. In front of a splendid "rocaille" fireplace Baroness Matilde Anyos Crespi, an exceptional model, posed with two of Carosa's creations: a dramatic cape of velvet lined with beige cloth worn over a classic dinner dress of black jersey, and a formal evening dress in Matisse pink chiffon with a pearl-encrusted bodice. Surrounded by incunabula, *trompe-l'oeil* and old and modern canvases, Irene Brin herself was photographed wearing a black jersey dress by Carosa.[18]

A few months later the galleria served as the set for a service on the hats of the milliner Clelia Venturi: the Tuscan straw trimmed with wild flowers presented curious and vague affinities with the lines of the hats, the people and the clothes depicted in the celebrated posters of Toulouse-Lautrec on show at the Obelisco. It was a play of allusions and reflections that was proposed to the reader of *Bellezza*,[19] who, looking at the beautiful photos of Pasquale De Antonis, found herself confusing the models wearing Venturi's creations with Lautrec's Parisian celebrities: May Belfort and Yvette Guilbert. An experience that grew even more complicated in the pages of *Images de Lautrec*, the catalogue of the exhibition on the French painter held at the Obelisco in the spring of 1947, where Irene Brin had conceived a rapid fictionalization of the figures illustrated.

Something similar happened on the occasion of the staging of *Come vi piace*, the Italian version of Shakespeare's *As You Like It* directed by Luchino Visconti and with scenery and costumes by Salvador Dalí, at the Teatro Eliseo on November 26, 1948. The costumes were made at the Mangili Palmer couture house, which had moved to Via Frattina in Rome several years earlier, keeping up the sartorial tradition of the Milanese atelier that had been destroyed during the bombing of the city. In those years Irene Brin was keeping an eye on developments at the Roman fashion houses, studying not just the collections but also the milieu and the clients. She had always appreciated the exquisite skills of the Mangili Palmer atelier and had a particular affection for her deceased friend, Marta Palmer:

[...] she was not just a dressmaker, but a friend, and the mark that she was unable to leave on the style of her time, [...] can be found in the memory of all those who, like Alberto Savinio, think back on her house, on the warmth of her life, on the intensity of what she had to offer, as a demonstration of human capacities.[20]


The fashion house was still in the hands of Eva Mangili[21] who kept the memory of Marta alive as death had been forbidden to enter it. The atelier was frequented by the actresses Isa Miranda, Neda Naldi and Kiki Palmer, Marta's daughter.
The article "Salvador Dalí in sartoria" ("Salvador Dalí at the Dressmaker's") conveys all the complexity of the passage from the artist's sketch to the making of the costume. Dalí's artistic eccentricity had to be translated into practical terms through the technical and craft skills and creativity of Eva Mangili, called on to make that surrealist fantasy fit the bodies of the actors, and the needs of their performance. It is not so much on the difficulty of this passage – a familiar problem when making the costumes for a play – that attention is focused, as on the discovery of how this exercise of translating the sketch into the hybrid, disquieting and circumstantial character of fashion was congenial to the artist Dalí, with his lively and sparkling imagination.

When Dalí came here [to the Mangili Palmer atelier] for the first time and sat, dressed in black, on the yellow sofa with its soft and familiar springs, he looked even more unusual and premeditated than he would have done in a hotel lobby, in a Roman tavern, in one of the castles of the Campagna. Calculated to the millimeter, with his cane, the pearl on his necktie, the pointed ends of his moustache. [...] He was there to give Eva the designs of the costumes ordered from him by Luchino Visconti: Shakespeare translated into a refinement in which old surrealism almost attacked a very young baroque. Borromini, plus *Vogue*, Bernini, plus *Harper's Bazaar*. [...] Salvador Dalí cannot limit himself to merely setting out his theories on contemporary painting in public: he always prefers to present himself to his audience enclosed in a diving suit, with two greyhounds on a leash, or with a loaf of bread several meters long on his head. In the same way his inventions for *As You Like It* are based on the outward need to astonish, and on the very private desire to create masterpieces.[22]

Audacity, farsightedness and above all a congenial feeling for fashion allowed the journalist to discern in Dalí's costumes an alchemical continuity from Borromini and Bernini to *Vogue* and *Harper's Bazaar*. Perhaps not so much because – we speculate – a suggestive affinity between the helmet crowned with branches he designed for *As You Like It* and the way that the hair of Bernini's *Daphne* metamorphoses into foliage had taken shape in her mind, as in virtue of the profound affinity linking the sense of fashion with surrealism and the baroque. Even in our own day, Gilles Deleuze has explored the figurative, and philosophical, connection between fashion and the baroque in *The Fold*.[23]

We do not know whether Irene Brin was familiar with Simmel's essay on fashion, but it is interesting here to quote the passage from it devoted to the relationship between fashion and the baroque. In the light of Simmel's ideas the journalist's observations take on the significance of a contribution to the theoretical foundations of the culture of fashion.

In contrast [to the classical] everything that is baroque, lacking restraint, outward, is intimately linked to fashion; for things that have these characteristics fashion does not come as a destiny imposed from the outside, but as the historic expression of their objective qualities. The widely projecting limbs in baroque statues seem to be in perpetual danger of being broken off, the inner life of the figure does not dominate them completely but abandons them to the relationship with the fortuitousness of the outer being. Baroque figures, or at least many of them, already have within them the restlessness, the fortuitous character, the subjection to the momentary impulse that fashion produces as a form of social life.[24]

That fashion was a favorite field of expression for the surrealist avant-garde was a well-known fact in the thirties, and Brin herself had devoted a paragraph of the entry "Surrealism" in *Usi e Costumi 1920-1940* to this mutual fascination:

[...] Signora Schiaparelli, couturière, embraced contemporaneously surrealism, Max Ernst and Dalí, asking them for furniture in the shape of women, tables supported by legs sheathed in black silk, hearts in cages: on few occasions has such a rapid and total decadence been seen, with ready-to-wear lines immediately appropriating sprouting violoncellos and headless manikins and de Chirico, in desperation, devoting himself to academic painting.[25]

But Irene Brin did not content herself with dedicating an article to the theatrical event at the Eliseo: she staged an exhibition of Dalí's designs at the Obelisco and edited its catalogue, contributing to it a note entitled *Complicità con Dalí* ("Connivance with Dalí"). The connivance is with the Dalí reviled by others, the very one that roused the "writer" in her by accumulating in his pictures

the myths of our time, those deserts adorned with bones, those tangles of snakes, those women with distant eyes and torn clothes, and closed doors, the spectral floors, amorous monsters, disquieting eagles and in short everything that oscillates between Freud and Mae West, between Brueghel and the covers of *Vogue*, between James Joyce and the Marx Brothers.[26]

THE MEETING WITH BRUNETTA MATELDI

When Brunetta Mateldi[27] came to Rome from Milan to illustrate the collections of the Roman fashion houses, Irene Brin took the opportunity to propose to the readers of *Bellezza* not just the presentation of the new lines as they were perceived by the "clinical" eye of her friend Brunetta, but also her acquaintance with the Savinio family home.

For her writing about fashion was not so much the recognition of a merely sartorial reality as a spur to a broadening of the perceptual space in which the connection between production and consumption could be grasped. Thus, in her presentation of Brunetta, the figure of the illustrator was set in a narrative frame: through the filter of the variations in the weather, of the alternation of sun and rain, using visual methods that are reminiscent of impressionist technique. A direct emotional communication was established between Brunetta's persona and the reader. Looking back on it today, one has the impression of an inchoative, polysemous mode of narration, not rigidly structured but repackagable and reproducible according to need.

Owing to its photographic and serial character, that budding persona could, for example, serve to represent the typical image of the foreign tourist in Rome in the fifties, set against the evocative backdrop of Trinità dei Monti, just as it would actually be used shortly afterward on the set of the movie *Roman Holiday*. Or in *The Roman Spring of Mrs. Stone*, based on Tennessee Williams's novel.

Brunetta arrived in Rome with the sun, and we all thought that it suited her a great deal. We would have liked to put her on the bottom steps of Trinità dei Monti and leave her there, to enjoy the heat, the stalls, the people, completing the morning scene with her fragile appearance, sensitive enough to the cold to make us feel the warmth of the air, petite enough to contrast with the voluptuousness of Roman women, and with those marvelous eyes wide open in their effort to understand everything, to make everything understandable to others. But the next day it rained and naturally Brunetta was even better suited to the damp, the reflections of the headlights on the wet sidewalks, the rush, a tired sadness that only she knew immediately how to turn around, to transform into the comfort of a conversation in front of the fire: it is true that, between one downpour and the next, she put away her beautiful umbrella with a black leather handle.[28]

One cannot fail to notice, in this passage, the irony with which the imaginary correspondence between character and weather is treated. The bizarre parallels between furnishings and unconventional styles of living in the house of the Savinio family are picked up and conveyed to us with the same "surreal" humor. We could say that she photographs the rooms with her pen in the same way as Brunetta portrays them with her pencil:

[...] the Savinio family have a house that resembles a game of mah-jongg, without certainties or difficulties. There are two or three purposes and uses for each thing: the sofas turn into beds, the chests of drawers become desks, the dining room a study, the study a living room, the children's room has a shape unknown to textbooks of geometry, with corners, circles and little squares desired, it's not clear why, by the architect, and then sharpened or rounded off by the children themselves. These children, to stick to the rules of the game, turn out to be unexpectedly different: Angelica may be still at school, but she is engaged, Ruggero may be a boy scout, but he paints better than his father and his uncle.[29] [...] My affection and my admiration for Maria Savinio are sentiments so well known that I always feel embarrassed to repeat them [...]. I will say for the last time that she is blonde, pink and ageless, so that she gives a pleasing impression of eternity. We are in the times of the first "Omnibus," we are in the times of Eleonora Duse, of Pirandello, of the Teatrino Odescalchi, of the last tours in America, where Maria was a young actress. And she has kept the part, she always will, and Savinio preserves it for her, wailing "Maria!" every five minutes in amazed, love-stricken reproach. Brunetta draws them both surreptitiously, from behind a screen of dishes, of glasses: you can tell that she is happy, on vacation and liberated for an evening from the need to repeat a button, every encrustation, free to abandon herself to the joy of discovery, around perfect human faces.[30]

In the Roman ateliers Irene Brin observed the way Brunetta approached the new models, her extraordinary ability to capture the novelty of a line with the enthusiasm of someone who, despite having seen and drawn thousands of garments, thousands of accessories, still knows how to take a "gamble" with the monstrous goddess of appearances:

There is a sort of enormous wager between Brunetta and Fashion: that immense, ponderous octopus that only a superficial observer could mistake for the enchantress Alcina. The monster with its innumerable hats, its innumerable claws sheathed in stockings or gloves or bedecked with rings, tries to choke Brunetta, to suffocate her in boredom and dreariness, and she defends herself with innocence, sincerely taking pleasure in Frattegiani's sandals, the Boutique's gloves, Luciana's jewelry.[31]

The various fashion houses parade their collections: Battilocchi, Antonelli, Gattinoni, Visconti, Mangili Palmer, Fontana. And even the unexpected happens, when Brunetta is moved to tears by the latest creations of the milliner Clelia Venturi:

[...] but at Clelia Venturi's a kind of miracle takes place. Brunetta's eyes turn bright with tears, the approving tears of a connoisseur, of a great worker, of an expert. It is the quality of the work, of the inspiration that moves her, almost dryly: the plum-black beret, the beret with mignonette and feathers, the beret in rosewood plush, have for her the importance of a model machine, of exemplary pictures, and she plays with the curves of the brim, with the alternation of the feathery reflections, disinterested and happy.[32]

The affinity between the work of the illustrator and that of the milliner brings out the creativity of both, based on know-how, on expertise, on the capacity to give rise to a style that is not exhausted in the realization of the object, but prefigures the features of its future protagonist. The garment and the accessory are born with the personage, with the figure of the woman who will wear them in the boutiques, in the salons, in the galleries. Brunetta with her uncut sketchbook, just purchased from Pineider on Via Due Macelli, will hurry to outline the portrait, conscious of the extent to which the characters of these circles are the latest incarnations of fictional types already shaped by literature: now steeped in irony, and ready to play the part of, if not creators of fashion, at least mannequins, who will soon have to leave the scene to very young professional models.

Besides the current beauties (and the future shadows) are waiting for Brunetta at the Galleria del Obelisco. They are so young, so fragile, so perfect that they could easily fit into one of Stendhal's books. One would like to speak with the errors of spelling, syntax, heraldry and logic that render Clelia and Vanina so exquisite: *la ravissante Basolina, la délicieuse Wolkonska... Cette jeune princesse Napolitaine, dont la mère... On se souvient que l'oncle de cette grande duchesse Moscovite...*[33]

JOURNEYS: PROMOTION OF ITALIAN FASHION IN THE WORLD

So Rome *caput mundi* for fashion too? In that moment the answer was yes. And Irene Brin made herself the ambassadress of Italian fashion to the four corners of the earth.

On June 2, 1955, the honor of Cavaliere Ufficiale dell'Ordine al Merito della Repubblica Italiana (Knight Officer of the Order of Merit of the Italian Republic) was bestowed on Irene Brin, in recognition of her efforts as a journalist, in Italy and abroad, to promote the development and success of Italian fashion in the world. Because of her cosmopolitan background, she had been often been given the task of choosing the most representative fashion houses to be sent to expositions staged overseas. The first was the one held in March 1952 at Punta del Este, which she supervised personally, going to South America with the models and designers she had selected.

The occasion was unique as it was the first time a foreign country had put on an event at which French and Italian fashion were in direct competition. The contest looked like being an unequal one and the journalist's diplomatic and organizational talents turned out to be of considerable importance: conscious of the superiority of French fashion, she took care to make sure that Italy was represented by the houses that enjoyed the most international prestige.

In the opinion of the French (and in the opinion of the Italians), it was nevertheless an unequal contest. French fashion has a superiority over ours which no one doubts, least of all ourselves: tradition, preparation, organization, those precise, bureaucratic and infallible forces which out of pure affectation the French disguise with high-sounding phrases, "*le goût de Paris, le ciel de Paris, le chic de Paris.*" Italian fashion counts chiefly on its inferiority: gaiety, inspiration, courage, those youthful, inexhaustible and lively forces which, out of pure affectation, the Italians hide behind timid phrases like "Improvisation, hot sun, good quality."[34]

The event, a long way away from the major European and American markets for fashion, was more of a challenge for Italy than for its rival France. Irene Brin was well aware that the exposition was one of innumerable important tests for a country that had long been isolated. It was only a few seasons earlier that Italian fashion had embarked on the relentless course of growth and promotion that was to lead to the triumph of the Italian look at the end of the seventies. For weeks the success of the exposition was threatened by a snub from the major couturiers of Paris, unwilling to countenance a contest between France and Italy: it was only when Germaine Lecomte, a modest figure in the world of *haute couture*, agreed to take part, promising to bring with her an anthology of the creations of Fath and Dior, that the initiative got off the ground. Although these new conditions made up for the initial imbalance between French and Italian fashion, difficulties remained, largely owing to the fact that Lecomte showed models that were already very well known and had for months occupied the pages of the most widely read fashion magazines in features with titles like "Caprices and Oddities" or "Follies of the World." The clothes of Dior, Balenciaga and Fath were certainly a great success, but Lecomte's choices wounded the sensibilities of Uruguayan women who, under a very simple exterior, showed a refined taste, coached in the elegance of Deauville and the Venice Lido. The Uruguayans chose "Italian clothes, Italian models and, evidently, Italian prices, with absolute freedom of spirit" because they were able to appreciate the qualities of those creations: "the fresh proposals, the unexpected combinations of colors, the charm of the Italians."[35]

In the meantime, in that same June of 1955, Italian fashion was preparing to land in Sydney, for an event called the "Italian Parade." When the buyers of David Jones, an Australian chain of department stores, had gone to Florence in the month of January for the presentation of the collections, operators in the sector, including journalists, had felt a particular need to bring their professional skills to bear, not just in view of the opening up of a possible new market but also because of the interest shown in them by internationally established figures. On this occasion, the work of promoting Italian fashion did not assume emphatic and triumphalist tones in *Bellezza*. Irene Brin always acted with discretion: aware of the real value of national production, she did not underestimate the requirements of the country for which the "made in Italy" was destined. Her words were intended to stress the importance of that exchange and the creative potentialities inherent in every new encounter: Italian fashion, along with the sectors of luxury automobiles and interior design, became part of the lifestyle of a faraway country, characterized by its cultural diversity, that for Italy had been and still was a land of emigration.

We certainly don't want to shout "Italian fashion a total triumph in the antipodes too!" for we are aware of our limits and the resources of others. We know that Australian women are sophisticated, that the country's stores are richly stocked and that Australian handicrafts are interesting. It is precisely for this reason we are delighted that complements, suggestions and alliances should set off for Australia from our country, and we see, in the clothes chosen to represent our taste down under, messages of friendship and cooperation. Our favorite among David Jones's many buyers is, let us admit it straightaway, a young woman whose parents are Italian but who was brought up in Australia, Marisa Martelli. In her delicate persona, in her tranquil and measured efficiency, we are happy to recognize a symbol of the most desirable fusion between two apparently different worlds. And we are glad that Marisa Martelli has selected a number of other contributions: the jewelry of Tre P, Rosa's lively dolls, perfumes, cosmetics and articles made of straw, and coral, and fabrics and toys, patiently exploring an Italy less familiar to the usual buyers.[36]

From the models in the collections for the summer of 1955 presented in Florence the Australian buyers chose a few examples of refined daywear designed by Schuberth, Capucci and Carosa: their preference was above all for comfortable and practical lines in cool cottons and soft jerseys, amongst which jackets and tunics with matching half-length pants were a hit. Another great success was the beach outfits with short skirts or pants and light jerseys, in a genuine riot of striped fabrics, made by La Tessitrice of Capri, whose handloom textiles had launched beachwear all over the world. Outstanding among the sixty-five models acquired by the buyers was the "quick-change outfit" devised by Antonelli: its reversible skirt, concealing matching pants, and top, accompanied by a pretty bolero, constituted an ideal getup for a variety of uses, and not just the beach. An interesting and picturesque collection designed specially for the Australian summer was the one by Emilio Pucci, who took his inspiration from the depths of the sea to create pantsuits in textilose cotton gabardine in shades of coral red and lobster pink, coupled with straw hats resembling giant underwater flowers.

Meanwhile the opportunities to encounter fashion produced abroad were increasing in Italy too, and in the fall of 1956 Venice, which had been the place chosen for the presentation of Italian collections several times in the past, proved once again to be the ideal city to stage the country's first international fashion event. The Rassegna Internazionale dell'Abbigliamento, dreamed up by the Centro delle Arti e del Costume then directed by Paolo Marinotti and free, at least at the outset, from aspects of a commercial nature, was staged at Palazzo Grassi.

The first International Fashion Show was conceived by the Center of Arts and Costume with a disarming ingenuousness, as if it were a poetry meet or a tournament. On each occasion, in Venice's Palazzo Grassi, the aim has been to follow the silk thread, to penetrate the heart of Venice, to find in a work of architecture or a fabric the explanation for a perpetually mysterious up-to-dateness. But no task was as momentous as this act of elegant alliance: inviting eight nations to show alongside Italy the clothes that they regarded as most representative of their way of life. In other words to propose to the whole world a cultural exchange of highly frivolous appearances.[37]

France turned down the invitation, but the Spanish and the Irish, direct rivals of Italy, took part in the event; as did the British and the Germans, solid in their development of the clothing industry; the Japanese and the Indians, confident in their exoticism; and the Americans, who did not fail to make a "show of their ostentation, their intelligence, their organization."[38]

Bettina Ballard, delegate of the USA and fashion editor of *Vogue*, paraded eighty garments chosen with taste and rigor, designed by Charles James, Valentina, Cassini and Pauline Trigère among others. The organization of the shows proved perfect not just in its timing, which entailed the presentation of around three hundred models on three consecutive evenings, but also in the friendly atmosphere that was created among the participants. The illustrator Brunetta Mateldi was appointed delegate for Italy and thanks to her competence and sense of humor succeeded in bringing out the qualities of Italian production, which ran the risk of appearing less rich than the American one, less surprising than the Spanish one and less striking than the Indian one. In short the comparison inevitably cast a shadow on the Italian proposals, which on top of it all suffered – as Irene Brin did not fail to point out – from "[...] a certain lack of discipline, a certain need to go it alone, invaluable when teamwork is not involved."[39] But the necessity to take care over the smallest detail, in order to attain the desired effect of discreet, but indispensable, reliability was understood.

Italy had few crinolines, few embroideries, few *coups de théâtre*. There was a deliberate attempt to avoid theatricalities in order to conform to the real traditions of refined women: the colors, the accessories, the contrasts were thought out with extreme patience, and Olga Asta wanted Maria Antonelli's "brides" to have fresh flowers every evening in the bouquets made out of her lace. [...] Catello D'Auria dyed whole pieces of leather to obtain shades identical to wools and silks, themselves often dyed to blend into a single tone; Dal Cò created thirty pairs of shoes; Giuliana Camerino came up with completely new handbags, despite making preparations to leave for Dallas, where she was to receive the Fashion Award.[40]

Thanks to the dedication of the operators, the show proved a great success and ushered in the practice, later taken up in many countries, of inviting creators of fashion from other nations. Among the fashion

designers who were establishing a reputation on the international
market for luxury goods were Germana Marucelli and Giovanna
Fontana.

Following the activity of Italian couturiers now requires a lot of patience, a good
grasp of geography and a sense of timing. Soon we are going to have to put a huge
map of the world up on the wall and stick little flags onto it: Faraoni is in Teheran,
Schuberth in Johannesburg, Emilio Pucci at St. Moritz, Roberto Capucci in
Stockholm, a Ferdinandi is at San Remo, two Fontanas in Pittsburg, Simonetta and
Fabiani are awaited in Tokyo, Olga de Grésy has just left Tahiti... And we could on
practically forever: a cheerful courage is prompting our creators to take on not just
unknown lands, but unfamiliar tastes, trusting to their instinct as if it were a wind.[41]

The expansion that Italian fashion underwent in the fifties and its
success on the scene of international *couture* was not simply the export
of a style, of a material culture, but the expression of a sensibility and
know-how capable of translating into clothing the specific
requirements of women in other countries, from New York to
Caracas.[42] The idea of including in the collections models aimed at
mass consumption as well as the elite, exportable to those nations
where ready-to-wear lines were in demand for distribution through
the chain stores, was gaining ground. All this entailed a series of
changes in the approach to dressmaking, commencing with the need
to experiment with new crease-resistant, sun-fast fabrics with a high
percentage of nylon in its various diverse forms, such as lace and
Terital, for light, practical clothing that required little attention: in
short, clothing capable of putting up with the inconveniences of
rapid travel. Synthetic materials became popular and the great
couturiers began to explore new criteria in their combinations of
garments and in adapting them to functions different from the
traditional ones.
I am reminded of a jade green shawl made by Antonio De Luca on
the occasion of Irene Brin's round-the-world tour in the spring of
1959. What had been conventionally regarded as an accessory was
now transformed into a garment that wrapped right around the bust
and hung down behind for the entire of the dress as a replacement for
the cape and even for the evening coat.[43]
It is just one example of a much broader effort to rationalize and

simplify the wardrobe for a specific purpose. The process was destined to grow more radical: in time it would profoundly revolutionize the conception of traveling clothes: we are thinking of the "Torchon" travel wear by Nanni Strada, one of the most original inventions of Italian design in the eighties.

In the article "Viaggi ben organizzati e guardaroba internazionali" ("Well-Organized Journeys and International Wardrobes"), Irene Brin, her gaze turned on the creations of *haute couture*, still aimed at an elite, explained how in the wardrobe of a star on a world tour a sumptuous mantle of rhodia[44] could become a *robe d'intérieur* suitable for receiving the press, or how a dress made of midnight blue rhodia shantung could prove ideal any evening from six o'clock onward, in New York as in Paris, or in any other place, as it was capable of responding precisely to known or unforeseeable circumstances. Accessories were also designed to meet all the needs of a life on the move: Luciana's jewelry had the consistency of feathers; Cleo Romagnoli's hats had grown light and flexible; Dal Cò's pumps had never been so flimsy. The range of colors made it possible to carry a single handbag – red in youthful wardrobes, black in more austere ones – by Giuliana di Camerino, who

designed a second one for nights spent on aircraft, of a size permitted by the regulations, complete with robe, slippers, inner pocket for jewelry, outer pocket for documents, purse for cosmetics, compartment for detective novel and container for golden clutch bag, which will take the place of the handbag in the evening.[45]

And again the article declared that De Luca's blue coat dress was an essential part of any wardrobe: without the white collar it could be worn under the cape, without the jacket it became a sun dress and, combined with jewelry, turned into a dinner or cocktail dress:

The clothes that we reproduce here are, invariably, interchangeable, if not completely transformable. The small suit will be able to leave the neck free, to be worn with a high-necked sweater or with a striped blouse. None of the fabrics need ironing. In short, while we wait for the difficulties that will be posed by interplanetary journeys, De Luca has solved all the ones that we are faced with for the time being.[46]

De Luca was soon to realize that, precisely as a result of the ever more widespread vogue for travel, fashion could no longer limit itself to creating wardrobes based strictly on the dominant dress code of individual nations. Gianna Manzini recounts how the designer aspired to create collections endowed with the flexibility necessary to reflect what was emerging on the international panorama. The increasingly common practice of travel – along with the theater, cinema and literature – had contributed to the spread of images of beauty that lay outside the conventional European model, and fashion could not avoid taking account of the modifications made to "our" concept of beauty and elegance by the styles of dress of women from different continents:

Today, the woman, whatever country she may be from, is a strange mixture – on the level of taste and personality – of totally up-to-date ideas and influences from all over the world. [...] in my clothes, I have tried to reflect whatever is least spectacular, more perceptive and graceful in this panoramic "all over the world."[47]

But rather than an eclectic internationalism, this aspiration to a universal language on the part of fashion required from De Luca an effort of invention: the invention of a technique capable of making those influences work directly on the structural parts of the garment: "It's through technique," declared to Gianna Manzini, "that I strive to gain control of, if not exactly to attack, what has flashed through my mind as a poetic fantasy."[48]

NOTE_____

[1] Irene Brin, "Biancheria di ieri e di oggi," in *Bellezza*, no. 4 (1960), p. 72.
[2] *Ibid.*
[3] Gio Ponti, "È superfluo il superfluo?" in *Bellezza*, no. 1 (1945), p. 41.
[4] Irene Brin, "Il Nord e il Sud," in *Bellezza*, no. 1 (1945), pp. 61-2, 72.
[5] Roland Barthes, "From Gemstones to Jewellery," in Id., *The Language of Fashion*, ed by Andy Stafford, Michael Carter. New York-Oxford: Berg, 2006, p. 63.
[6] Irene Brin, "Il Nord e il Sud," in *Bellezza*, cit.
[7] *Ibid.*
[8] Bettina Ballard, *In My Fashion*. New York: David McKay Company, 1960, pp. 187-8.
[9] *Ibid.*
[10] Vinicio Marinucci, "Vetrine," in *Bellezza*, no. 35, (1943), pp. 44, 58.
[11] *Ibid.*
[12] Émile Zola, *Au Bonheur des Dames* (1883); Engl. ed. *Au Bonheur des Dames (The Ladies' Delight)*, trans. by Robin Buss. New York: Penguin Classics, 2002.
[13] Cf. Elizabeth Wilson, *Adorned in Dreams. Fashion and Modernity*. London: Virago, 1985, pp. 144-54.
[14] Irene Brin, "Passeggiata romana," in *Bellezza*, no. 7 (1946), pp. 16-19.

[15] *Ibid.*

[16] *Ibid.*

[17] Irene Brin, "Massima e Minima," in *Bellezza*, no. 4 (1946).

[18] Irene Brin, "Un altro Obelisco," in *Bellezza*, nos. 12-13 (1946), pp. 22-3.

[19] Irene Brin, "Alla Toulouse Lautrec," in *Bellezza*, nos. 18-19 (1947), pp. 24-5.

[20] Irene Brin, *Usi e Costumi 1920-1940*, Rome: Donatello De Luigi, 1944, pp. 61-2.

[21] Particular attention was paid to Eva Mangili, expert creator of theatrical costumes, by Gianna Manzini in the article "Abiti per la ribalta. Tra vestiti che ballano" published in *La Fiera Letteraria* on February 13, 1947. The writer set out to underline how the dressmaker and designer became "a sort of 'driving value' who works in free collaboration with the playwright, and in a brilliant manner, very distant from that mere juggling with a scheme which is typical instead of those who are tied to immediate practical aims." (Gianna Manzini, "Abiti per la ribalta. Tra vestiti che ballano," in Id., *La moda di Vanessa*, ed. by Nicoletta Campanella. Palermo: Sellerio Editore, 2004, p. 229).

[22] Irene Brin, "Salvador Dalí in sartoria," in *Bellezza*, no. 1 (1949), pp. 58-60.

[23] Gilles Deleuze, *Le Pli* - Leibniz et le baroque (1988). Eng. trans. by Tom Conley, *The Fold*. Minneapolis: University of Minnesota Press, 1992.

[24] Georg Simmel, "Fashion," (1904) in D. Levine (ed. by), *Georg Simmel*. Chicago: University of Chicago Press, 1971. The passage cited here has been translated from the Italian ed., *La Moda*. Milan: Mondadori, 1996, p. 63.

[25] Irene Brin, *Usi e Costumi 1920-1940*, cit., p. 14.

[26] Irene Brin, "Complicità con Dalí", in *Come vi piace* (*As You Like It*), in the version staged by the Compagnia Italiana di Prosa, directed by Luchino Visconti. Rome: Carlo Bestetti Edizioni d'Arte, 1948.

[27] Brunetta Mateldi (1904-88). An outstanding illustrator of Italian fashion for the magazine *Bellezza*, Brunetta was an unusual figure in the sector of the illustration of society and fashion journalism. For the versatility of its graphic style, influenced by the lesson of impressionist drawing and the artistic innovations of the historical avant-garde movements, Brunetta's work was appreciated and sought after by the main exponents and operators of Italian and international fashion. Her drawings were not mere illustrations of the new collections, but genuine re-creations capable of capturing all the pregnancy of a new silhouette in a few sharp and penetrating lines, and of immediately setting it in an environmental and cultural situation. Brunetta's figures were real people living in a space with which they seemed to interact.

[28] Irene Brin, "Giornate romane fra pioggia e sole," in *Bellezza*, nos. 24-5 (1947), pp. 21-33.

[29] The famous painter Giorgio de Chirico. *Translator's note.*

[30] Irene Brin, "Giornate romane fra pioggia e sole," cit.

[31] *Ibid.*

[32] *Ibid.*

[33] *Ibid.*

[34] Irene Brin, "Italia a Punta del Este," in *Bellezza*, no. 4 (1952), pp. 70-2.

[35] *Ibid.*

[36] Irene Brin, "Partiti per l'Australia," in *Bellezza*, no. 6 (1955), pp. 42-53.

[37] Irene Brin, "Incontro internazionale della moda a Venezia," in *Bellezza*, no. 10 (1956), pp. 92-104.

[38] *Ibid.*

[39] *Ibid.*

[40] *Ibid.*

[41] Irene Brin, "Moda italiana giramondo," in *Bellezza*, no. 4 (1956), p. 124.

[42] *Ibid.*

[43] Irene Brin, "Ho scelto un guardaroba per il giro del mondo," in *Bellezza*, no. 5 (1959), pp. 62-4.

[44] "Rhodia" is an artificial fiber with a silky and shiny appearance, similar to organza, created in imitation of silk during the period of autarchy. *Translator's note.*

[45] Irene Brin, "Viaggi ben organizzati e guardaroba internazionali," in *Bellezza*, no. 6 (1957), pp. 46-7.

[46] *Ibid.*

[47] Gianna Manzini, "La moda tende a un linguaggio universale," in *La moda di Vanessa*, cit., p. 211.

[48] Ivi, p. 212.

S. VISCONTI

Simonetta dresses. From Irene Brin, *Sole d'Italia in pieno inverno di New York*, in Bellezza, yr. XII, no. 2, February 1952. Courtesy Accademia di Costume e di Moda, Rome. Donated by Irene Brin

# THERE ΛRE NO SECRETS IN ΛMERICΛ

THE FORMULA OF AMERICAN FASHION

At the end of the Second World War, the American market became
of prime interest to Europe, which now had to reconsider its position
as a guide to elegance. North America was "the greatest consumer of
models,"[1] and Paris was unable to satisfy the demands of a market
that was opting for new standards of elegance for the masses. For
Italian fashion, which was making substantial inroads into areas that
were "remote" for the times, like South America and Australia, it
now became essential to attract the major buyers of the United States.
It was an opportunity to turn its late arrival on the scene into an
advantage, and to tackle ready-to-wear head on. So the way was
opened not only for an industrial and technological advance but also,
and this would be even more decisive for the future, for a genuine
revolution in the conception of dressmaking. It was the beginning of
the phase of modern research into methods of standardizing the
female figure, of presenting and exporting it, that was to have
incalculable consequences on ready-to-wear right down to our own
day.

The big American department stores – Bergdorf Goodman, Bonwit Teller, Henri Bendel, Saks, Altaman and Magnin – knew how to distill the most well calibrated and succinct formula for dressing American women from the fashion created in Europe. This formula was so carefully weighed that it was able to function for clothing at a high and middle level as well as at an economic one. The skill of the American garment makers lay in their capacity to utilize every aspect of the model, to break it down into its minimum terms and put it back together with small variations for its use in ready-to-wear. A model, like a text, could be translated into another language – it is no coincidence that in English the term can be used as a synonym for adaptation – and this striking process was not seen in any way as a "betrayal" of the original model but as a means of bringing out its virtuality. The fact that in the early fifties the most important department stores in the United States had a *haute couture* section dedicated to "Italian Fashion" was a clear sign of the prestige assigned to the country's dressmaking. Yet it had to be asked, as Elsa Robiola did ask, whether the exclusiveness of Italian collections did not at bottom conceal a difficulty in coming up with formulas that would permit a broader utilization of the models. In other words if the time had not come to give serious consideration, in view of future developments, to the message that came from "a country which does not dress like us, but takes ideas from us to counter the lesson of how we should dress in the future."[2] If the conception of dress most appropriate to the diverse lifestyles of the big American cities was that of the ready-to-wear formula, then there was every chance that the same idea of fashion would prove a success in the rest of the world.

MASS-PRODUCED BEAUTIFUL WOMEN

A few months prior to the historic event staged at Villa Torrigiani in Florence, Irene Brin drew attention to a point of tension between the American and European conception of fashion. The stringent system of defenses erected by Parisian couture against any form of prying had no counterpart in the United States:

There are no secrets in America, for any reason, for any season. Mrs. Sophie Gimbel, proprietor, director and no. 1 designer of Saks, left Italy in the first half of July to take refuge in an American villa and marina and prepare the 1951 spring collection, which she will show immediately after Christmas. She will have no need to protect herself from the curiosity of her competitors, who in turn will show no interest in spying on her. If Mrs. Gimbel has decided, as she seem to have done, on the fabrics of Contessa Marinetta di Frassinetto, she will use kilometers and kilometers of them: if she chooses the canal line, or the mandolin line, she will churn out them out in vast numbers. Mass production, which is brought to its own level of perfection by the big fashion houses, such as Saks, ends up creating a very special climate [...].[3]

The figure of the couturier-artist agoraphobically at work in his or her atelier looked almost pathetic when compared with the free and confident actions of Mrs. Gimbel. In this case Irene Brin, who on other occasions was quite ready to welcome signs of the growing democratization of fashion, indulged in a hint of wistfulness, almost of nostalgia, and underlined the prescriptive character of mass production. She saw ready-to-wear as a new regime to which women once again found themselves "subjected":

The direct consequence of collective elegance is a collective, incomprehensible sadness and these wonderful American ladies who have swarmed all over Europe over the course of the summer seem to have gone back to the ancient custom of the national costume. The pinafores of the Tyrolese, the shawls of the Venetians, the bonnets of the Bretons have fallen out of use: but the migrations of American women to Europe are governed by injunctions more strict than any tradition. Last year they were all wearing capes of white taffeta; this year they're all wearing capes of black chiffon over dresses of pleated chiffon. [...] In just one evening at Caracalla, I counted thirty short, black evening-dresses that left the left shoulder bare; and fifty pairs of pumps in pale pink patent leather.[4]

The uniformity of these styles was brought into focus at a glance. Under her scrutiny their affinity with anachronistic regional costumes was clearly revealed. Indeed she seems not to have made any proper distinction between fashion and costume. Nor had she grasped the egalitarian lesson of Chanel's little black dress. Perhaps we can understand the reason for this "obtuseness" by referring to the article entitled "Fanno loro la vera moda (They Make the Real Fashion)" of 1949, where ready-to-wear provided the cue for a comparison between two different attitudes toward fashion. Central here was the figure of the "dressmaker," up until then a familiar, almost romantic presence in the culture of dress most widespread in the country. "Dressmakers sew in the bedroom, take measurements in the dining room, use movie stars as their models. Their charges are very modest, and so their glory is more definitive than that of Fath or Dior"[5] – declares the subtitle of the article, in a markedly quixotic and sentimental tone, notwithstanding the lucidity implied in the identification of the theme.

The women of Northern Europe believe in mass production. It is an arid but stern myth, that permits few illusions, and in compensation limits disappointments, giving monotony the bitter taste of impeccability. 'Round each campus, cross the nation – the smart girl dresses in Swirl' declares the publicity for the check dress (9 dollars) targeted at all female students at all American universities. And if they use it, the advertisement must be effective, even if we find it incomprehensible.

"The women of the South believe in dressmakers. It is another myth, of course, and a dangerous one because it allows disasters of the worst kind. A heartwarming one, however, and splendid. We have all grown up hearing the whir, in the spare room, of the sewing machine and the voice of the elderly widow who 'came by the day.' In a whisper, she was assigned extraordinary qualities, marred by terrible defects: 'What a pity she drinks, because otherwise she sews like an angel! You have to keep an eye on the reels of thread, sometimes she steals them, but then again...' She is an almost vanished figure: the daughters of the widow hired for the day have usually decided to go and work for some large couture house, and they are unlikely to ever stop, as they acquire an arid pride, comparable to that of the domestic servants of the aristocracy, and prefer spending their whole lives sewing humble whipstitches in an illustrious workshop to creating ball gowns for a middle-class family.[6]

It is as if Brin were torn between impersonating the role of the fashion journalist, careful to report the smallest change in the world of couture, and that of the writer, who in a squint-eyed manner divides her attention between the real subject and its fictional shadow.

My favorites are the independent, isolated [dressmakers], who live on the wrong side of the railroad tracks and do their sewing in the bedroom, their measuring in the dining room (there is always a big table, with a lace cross and an aspidistra in a brass pot, and the light trembles as the trucks go past). In the next room the invisible presence – but given away by a husky voice, the rustle of newspapers, the opening of a drawer – of a lover, a husband or a lodger, lends a sinister tone, that of a song by

Edith Piaf. Will she come to a sticky end, stabbed or strangled, this slovenly seamstress, with her hair falling in her eyes, and the hem of her skirt unstitched? In the meantime she is cloaked in the possibility of a miracle: and she is not punctual, and not precise, and accepts neither suggestions nor criticisms. If you take her a fashion magazine, she barely glances through it, unwillingly, lingering only on the pages of advertisements, looking at the colorful, gaudy and impracticable pictures. If you give her a well-cut garment that a friend has allowed you to copy, she picks it up with two fingers, condemns it in silence, lets it fall. She accepts suggestions only from the cinema, and from American movies: Loretta Young and occasionally Joan Crawford are the people who inspire her. Here prices are unpredictable. Sometimes she turns up late in the evening to demand, severely, payment of a bill of 1500 lire for a skirt. Another time she puts off for six months the effort of writing down, on a bit of paper of dubious cleanliness, 'Making. Prinsess dress 6000 lire, zipper 380 lire, padding 1200 lire, various materials 75 lire.'

She may decide to become rich and famous, and succeed. More often she chooses anonymous poverty, but it is always her, confused, violent and sensitive, who governs fashion.[7]

Is it plausible that it was the impossibility of extending the scope of the narrative to the life of the beautiful and elegant but still unknown American women who wore off-the-rack clothes that made the thirty short black dresses with the shoulder left bare she saw on a summer evening at Caracalla appear, ahistorically, mere replicas of Tyrolese pinafores and Venetian shawls? And how much influence did Hollywood portrayals of the female figure have on the inhibition of her storytelling vein?

Emilio Cecchi had lucidly pointed out how American illustrated magazines and movies were "unparalleled in their neutralization of the female body as well; in the way they strip it of spirit and commotion, turning it into rubber."[8] What were represented were fragments of the female body, with a uniformity and a monotony that reflected how the human body had been "rendered abstract by mass production."[9] Seen from this particular viewpoint, the degree of standardization of the female figure was a complex indication of the drift toward alienating homogeny that could result from the democratization of consumption. Irene Brin had expressed her own suspicions about the consumption of mass-produced articles in the passage in *Usi e Costumi 1920-1940* entitled "The Department Stores":

In New York, in the 'Clothing' department, customers often served themselves, without the assistance of salesgirls but almost automatically, following the indications of posters, numbers and luminous signs, picked out clothes that they tried on, by themselves, in front of the mirror, brushing against other women, equally alone, equally lost in their own image, wavering between the emerald green jacket and the cypress green jacket. [...] Everyone felt anonymous, very up-to-date and unhappy. Chagall and Ringelnatz seemed to be the real prophets of the Department Stores.[10]

This explains why she felt that La Rinascente and Upim were destined to import into Italy the same state of solitude that characterized large-scale American consumption: ready-to-wear clothing entailed a loss of creativity, here gloomily described as an "unhappiness" on the part of the consumer, who was deprived of the socially reassuring value of "distinction." However, the fact could not be ignored that at that moment operators in the fashion industry found it necessary to carry out a radical reconfiguration of the complicated problem of communication linked to the practice of "distinction," moving in the direction of placing a greater emphasis, among broad strata of consumers, on the autonomy of Italian creativity, in contrast to the expressive subjection that some Roman collections still showed toward the catwalks of Paris.

The Italian couturiers have come back from Paris with an ambitious and incredibly monotonous booty, but one which they naively consider perfect. Out of the forty Roman collections at least twenty have shown Fath's dress with a long cravat hanging down to the hem of the skirt, and I began to carefully assemble photographs of the different versions. I was thinking of writing an article about them, to be sure, but also of making an art collection. All of us are masochists, now and then, and take delight in our own torments.[11]

A critical provocation tinged with a vein of irony permeates the whole article, and yet it does not fail to constructively point out the road Italian couture must go down in order to develop an original stylistic identity of its own, attractive to consumers at home and abroad. Her understanding of, constant attention to and unflagging contacts with international culture were instantly translated, in her writings, into invaluable suggestions about the strategy of image to be adopted.

Last month two great American photographers, Paul and Karen Radkai, again came to Rome to take pictures of the people and things considered important in America. They began, it is true, with the intellectuals Silone and Leoncillo, Moravia and Carlo Levi, Luchino Visconti and Suso d'Amico, Dario Cecchi and Cesare Zavattini, perhaps drawing on too obvious a source of information, an almost elementary culture that excluded the names of the very young, of the not-yet-translated, of the not-yet-exhibited, but in any case they turned to reliable forces, to well-recognized values. The difficulties began when the jewels, the ceramics of Valle dell'Inferno or the fabrics of Marinetta di Frassinetto were exhausted and they moved on to fashion.[12]

The fashion which Irene Brin was referring to here was not the Roman *haute couture* publicized in the magazines by photos of beautiful ladies of the aristocracy, which bore very Italian signatures, but the one that came out of the dismal dressmaker's shops which, at the end of March, still vegetate "in a dreary lethargy." These workshops overflowed with embroidered dresses capable of finding fortune only in some South American banana republic and the mannequins, still chilled by the rigors of the winter, mended stockings in the deserted salons. It was an allusion intended to underline the need to create a continuity between the fashion of the most prestigious atelier and the work of the minor dressmakers since, in Irene Brin's view, they ought to share those characteristics of imagination and handcrafted refinement that constituted without a shadow of doubt a great resource for the country.

Karen Radkai photographed for her newspaper and acquired for herself only those works of the couturiers that she found 'sufficiently Italian': and she must have used this phrase, in essence definitive, almost continually, and it could become a motto for our high fashion, certainly not for reasons of patriotism or rigor, which would become irritating, but out of calculation, out of astuteness, the need to be sensible. Karen Radkai's personal acquisitions could symbolize and summarize those of all American women in Italy: large, soft leather bags, in Florence and Rome. In Florence and Rome, again, comfortable, agreeable and inexpensive shoes. Fabiani's suit in green wool, with a black belt. Fontana's light and dark outfit. The low-necked and sleeveless dress of black wool, but enlivened by a few jewels from Gabriellasport. The two little shantung dresses from Gattinoni. Dozens of scarves and shawls from the Tessitrice dell'Isola. Cerri's blouses. Franco Bertoli's sweaters. Gucci's umbrellas. The fabrics of Gegia Bronzini. The buckets of Giuliana Camerino. She liked our artisans, our hairdressers. She liked everything that matched an image which was indeed established in advance, but at the same time suggested very new possibilities. That Italy is now enjoying an almost romantic vogue, we all know: and so let us try to keep it that way, by deserving it.[13]

Italian fashion at the end of the forties was not yet able to make a conscious assessment of itself and was in need, in order to see itself as a positive entity, of an external perspective that could assemble its characteristic traits into a whole. Radkai's photographic gaze, so skillfully and succinctly described by Irene Brin, was offered here as a visual device, as a means of obtaining a still elusive image of identity, still too fragmented and incoherent to be presented in its own right. It was not until the beginning of the sixties that Irene Brin was able to note the presence, in Italy too, of those modes of consumption which, following in the footsteps of Chanel and her little black dress, would oblige ready-to-wear to appeal to a creativity capable of transcending, in the imagination, the purely material fact of the garment.

Designers propose, buyers dispose and women compose. It's a new proverb, but it is an apt one for fashion. And in fact twice a year the designers study lines and colors carefully, deluding themselves that they can in some way determine the future. Then the buyers arrive, even more ingenuous because they put their trust in statistics and arguments. Finally the ordinary girl, the beautiful, proud and well-rounded girl that we see in our streets, makes her choice and, taking one element from the boutique, another from *haute couture*, yet another from the old drawer and the final one from her own imagination, puts together something that the designers didn't create and that the buyers didn't see, but is her own innovation.[14]

THE GLAMOROUS COUNTESS
But in 1952, only two years after the article on off-the-peg elegance, her perspective had already changed. The occasion was provided by the presentation in New York of a collection by Simonetta Visconti, "the glamorous countess." The article "Sole d'Italia in pieno inverno di Nuova York" ("Italian Sun at the Height of Winter in New York")[15] recounts how Bergdorf and Goodman, for the "Golden Anniversary" of the department store, chose to show thirty-five models designed in Rome by Simonetta Visconti and intended for the

still far-off spring-summer season. The clothes conjured up a season steeped in Mediterranean allure, extremely remote and unlikely in a New York cloaked in winter fog. And yet fashion seduced by means of just these sudden and unexpected juxtapositions, and disorientations, which paved the way for a process of imagination, for accounts of potential existential opportunities, introduced in the fashion magazine by means of hackneyed openings: "… the striped shorts or the check one-piece garments looked like the magic mirrors of fortunetellers: you'll be like this if… you can dress like that when…"[16]

It was the beginning of a narrative spark – it could have been be the caption of the garment – that stemmed here from her observation and knowledge of Simonetta's history as a creator of fashion. The inventive line and the lively blend of colors of the models she prepared for the American market – *Caviar on Salmon* was the eloquent title of a dress in orange shantung with black buttons – were not all that remote, at the root, from the creativity she had showed amidst the distressing reality of the end of the war, when opening the small dressmaker's shop on Via Gregoriana had constituted an act of great courage on the *countess*'s part: "Rome just liberated from the Germans, and still subject to innumerable restrictions, lacked electric light as well as basting, fabric as well as sewing machines."[17]

Simonetta's first show in Rome had been a success that was half cheering and half touching. Irene Brin now recalled that success:

Simonetta had used dishtowels, linings, rustic headscarves, gardening smocks and the jackets of domestic servants and had made out of them eighteen masterpieces of inventiveness and practicality. Even though the beaches were mined, even though the pinewoods were still smoking and bunkers blocked the way to the sea, it was possible to believe again in vacations and freedom, looking at those sun dresses. Even now that she can rely on kilometers of tulle and carpets of mink, Simonetta Visconti remains faithful to such tricks of ingenious poverty. This summer she put ribbons to good account, now she's using embroidery inserts with eyelets. Straw for its part finds unusual possibilities and the Americans have applauded her large cloak of raffia, and underneath, a bodice also of raffia studded with emeralds, completed by a skirt of emerald green "aléoutienne." The knee-length pants are also made of raffia, with a double skirt in which curtain rings are the only ornament, and echo the touching confidence of 1945.[18]

ITALIAN ACTRESSES IN NEW YORK

The export of fantasies linked to different lifestyles was no longer, in the fifties, entrusted to the mere technology, however sophisticated, of the latest collection of clothes. With the growth in the number of people making intercontinental journeys, Italian fashion was now exported along with the celebrity image of culture and high society. The garment was not a model in a fashion plate, but a piece of clothing worn by someone, accompanied by a particular circumstance of existence and serving as a vehicle for intricate intercultural comparisons.

A week devoted to Italian cinema by the city of New York was the occasion for one of these comparisons. Italian actresses arrived in the future Big Apple, bringing with them a different lifestyle than that of American women; but they did not engage in competition with them, something that would have taken them on to too one-sided a terrain. Rather they set out to make the most of their difference, in ways that were wholly self-referential. The floodlight was turned on one aspect of that society: and the traditional tour by the Italian tourist through the "characteristic" areas of the American metropolis suddenly appeared devoid of interest.

The steamboat tour of the Manhattan peninsula in the morning; the ascent of the Empire State Building in the afternoon; the exploration of the deserted magnificence of Wall Street at night; and the visit, at any time, to the dinosaur in the Museum of Natural History. There are minor improvised variations: getting enthusiastic about Harlem and Chinatown, being disheartened by the Bowery. [...]. Yet no one will explain to the tourist that first of all he should invest a very large part of his capital in a lunch at the "Colony," the "Pavillion" or the "Aiglon."[19]

Irene Brin's suggestion was to devote your attention to those places, to those *milieux*, which offered an authentic testimony to the usages and customs of New York society:

These are not so much restaurants as dimly lit aquaria, where supple Italian waiters glide around laden with tropical fruit and espresso coffee percolators, where the bracelets of Cobiana Wright, the political opinions of Fleur Cowles and the aesthetic and equine expertise of Elizabeth Arden stand out.[20]

We are told in an ironic and worldly tone how these famous representatives of New York high society, together with a few dozen other "dominant women," meet up every day, around one o'clock, at tables where there is never a shortage of flowers and men, both of them always decorative and always silent: friends, secretaries, assistants and sometimes even husbands. At the Colony a rigorous style held sway, one which would be appropriated by the majority of American women: "a style of elegant matriarchy."[21]

It was from the Colony in New York, and certainly not from Paris, that the real orders came: wear little black or dark gray suits, tiny hats, three turns of a string of pearls, a fur stole and sunglasses over, at the most, 110 pounds of perfectly polished flesh, skin and bones. The new ballets of Lucia Chase, the new colors of mink, the new aid to Europe, everything was discussed and decided at the Colony by mature and highly competent women.

The three young Italian actresses who appeared on that stage, free from any desire to imitate, responded to this lifestyle in a totally independent way, without renouncing their own modes of being and appearing.

Three young Italian actresses, Silvana Mangano, Marina Berti and Eleonora Rossi-Drago (along with Elisa Cegani who separately achieved a success of her own), arrived in New York for the Week of Italian Cinema, engaged in, fought and probably also won a battle of which they were not even aware. It was the most ingenuous, the most unequal of struggles against the heroines of the Colony: and in fact the three actresses relied on just one stratagem, that of not painting their lips at all, of doing as little to their hair as possible and of applying makeup carefully to create the appearance of negligence. Beautiful all three, and accompanied by a friend so splendid that she was assumed to be Mangano's sister, whereas she was in fact the wife of the producer Ponti. No one ever saw them wear a hat, or the traditional little suit. No one saw them turn up on time for the appointments strictly made and strictly kept by American habits. No one ever heard them talk politics, nor for that matter of Marianne Moore or Barrault [...]. But who or what could have ruffled them, innocent and radiant as they were? Luckily they had not troubled to find out, perhaps by consulting *Reader's Digest*, about the moods and needs of the America they were about to face, the America of the Colony: so the momentous names of the essential hostesses, of the merciless reporters, of the authorized gossips, aroused in them neither enthusiasm nor dread. Doris Duke or Irving Penn, Cholly Knickerbocker or Anita Loos, left them equally unperturbed, as the fear and hope of being invited, described, photographed or placed at the heart of somebody's next novel did not even touch them. So everything worked out for the best. The stars attended the screening of seven movies, banquets and receptions. The enormous success of the event was attributed to them, who with luminous absentmindedness went on turning up late, not wearing hats, saying few words in English, not painting their lips. They passed through the fire of snobbism, waded the torrent of society rules and left triumphant: it was probably the only way of dealing with New York.[22]

The style of the three actresses left an indelible mark on the image that American society formed of the Italian look at that moment. Even in 1965, the magazine *Time*[23] still linked the success of Italian collections with the magnificent Roman women who had been its exceptional promoters. The article, written by Nina Borghese, pointed out how since the early fifties the female image proposed by Italian fashion had managed to supplant the classic representations of ideal femininity in the Anglo-Saxon world: the British lady and the sophisticated French *dame*, rigorously dressed in black.
Thus the simplicity of dress, the slightly disheveled hair and pale lips of the three Italian actresses – characteristics already glorified by the superb imagery of Anna Magnani – became specific and exclusive traits of that Italian look which was to hold its sway for a long time to come.


IMAGINING AMERICA

Irene Brin and her husband Gaspero del Corso were, in the early fifties, prominent figures on the Roman art scene and among the most receptive to the innovations to be found in the works of American artists. In the climate of cultural rapprochement between Italy and the United States – seen at that time as a symbol of freedom and dignity for the human condition – the world of contemporary art constituted one of the most fruitful areas of comparison: Rauschenberg, Calder and Gorky showed for the first time in Italy in the rooms of the Obelisco. Of particular interest to art historians is the Rauschenberg exhibition, entitled *Scatole e Feticci Personali* ("Contemplative Boxes and Personal Fetishes"), staged in March 1953. The show had given the American artist an opportunity to distance himself from the two-dimensional mode of pictorial expression:

The exhibition – Germano Celant would write – consisted of "boxes" in which the American artist had placed found objects, such as stones and bits of string, nails and hair, broken pieces of mirror and shell, containers and reproductions, pieces of wood and photographs that, following in the footsteps of Cornell, offered the first element in an investigation of the world and its found images.[24]

In June of the same year the Obelisco put on an exhibition called *Twenty Imaginary Views of the American Scene by Twenty Young Italian Artists*.[25] The works on show belonged to Helena Rubinstein, a close friend of del Corso's. The artists included Afro, with the work *Chicago*, Burri with *Jazz* and Mirko with a sculpture entitled *Los Angeles*. The catalogue, published by De Luca, contained a foreword by Rubinstein and an introduction by Alberto Moravia.

The works, commissioned by Rubinstein, who had been struck by the "singular inventiveness"[26] and the enthusiasm that many of these young artists displayed for developments on the other side of the Atlantic, were a response to her request that they represent, in a wholly imaginary way, the thing that attracted them most in that world. The result was extraordinary, as Rubinstein herself acknowledged, all the more so given that none of the twenty artists (with the exception of Burri who had been a prisoner of war at a camp in Hereford, Texas) had ever been to America. But then neither had Pavese and Vittorini ever seen the place.

In the introduction to the exhibition catalogue Alberto Moravia drew attention instead to the interest shown in Italian artists, at last free to express their vitality after the constraints imposed on them by the Fascist regime, which had confined them to a realm of "humiliating reticence and conformity."[27] The revelation of new forces of expression in the literary field as well as the visual arts and the cinema was baptized "the postwar Italian renaissance" in America: However, Moravia did not fail to point out that, in reality, the term "renaissance" was inappropriate. Rather than undergoing a complete interruption, artistic research in that period had gone underground like a karstic river and none of what surfaced after the war could really by seen as an improvised or extempore product.

THE FIGURE OF THE FASHION EDITOR

In the January of 1952 Carmel Snow, the charismatic fashion editor of *Harper's Bazaar*, arrived in Rome. Irene Brin gave an account, in the articles she wrote for *Bellezza*, of the encounters of this powerful figure in the American fashion publishing industry with the world of Roman *haute couture*, and with the society and cultural milieus of the capital. The journalist in her was literally fascinated by her American colleague, and the two of them embarked on a long friendship that was to lead to her becoming, a few months later, Rome editor for *Harper's Bazaar*. In this influential post, which she would hold until the end of her days, she would perform the function of talent scout of Roman and Italian fashion. It would be her job to select the most interesting models of the new collections and the material for publication to be sent to the American magazine. She might be entrusted with the preparation of a feature, the conception of a photographic set, the choice of the team that would assist her in her work. She would also be called on to promote the world of Italian art and culture in America and to serve as a point of reference for the magazine's correspondents in search of the "characteristic."

I found my first contacts with the Americans on fashion disconcerting because of the constant squandering of money. Hired cars, the most up-to-date cameras, films, rolls, assistants, accessories. Mountains of tissue paper that we Italians religiously keep together with big pins, fine pins and everything needed to puff out skirts or tighten a bodice.[28]

Irene Brin wanted to stress Snow's Irish temperament: a trait that, in her opinion, made her different from other magazine editors or famous women in the fashion world. She was impressed by the energy that was always ready to burst out, that emerged on the smooth surface of that face, sensitive as a photographic plate to the masterly and cultivated game of fragmentation and recomposition of deeply absorbed atmospheres and literary influences.

The little Carmel White (Snow was the name of her husband, rich, sporty, listed on the New York Social Register) was eternally an Irish girl after Joyce's own heart, a force of nature, a dainty bomber. She was born in Dublin in 1885. Her parents had later moved to the United States with the official assignment of promoting Irish handicrafts during one of the country's periodic rural crises. From Ireland she retained the accent, the sense of humor, the flashes of good cheer and fury. There was in her the same genius as Beckett, Brendan Behan, I would even say the terrible O'Neills, even Oscar Wilde and his mother, the misunderstood Lady Speranza.[29]

In her role as fashion editor, Carmel Snow is presented to us as a woman passionate about her job, who loved clothes and bought them unstintingly, surpassing even such an insatiable shopper as Elizabeth Taylor. But unlike the movie star, avaricious and full of uncertainty, Snow was not a prisoner of her clothes and got rid of them after about six months by offering them to the members of her editorial staff, who were thus able to get their hands, at a knockdown price, on a model by Balenciaga or Dior. The whole thing was done tactfully: she took pains to pin the roll of leftover material to the collar to allow for possible alterations. On her staff were the Bouvier sisters, who were to become famous as Jackie Kennedy and Lee Radzwill, always first in the rush to buy her castoffs. She ran the magazine strictly, but also with great patience. She kept a close eye on novices and did not fail to be severe even with the most famous of her collaborators: for example the photographer Richard Avedon, who on his last day of work for *Harper's Bazaar* was treated like a tyro and asked to do his feature over again. She was able to control her anger and express her disapproval in a simple way, although at times she could not manage to conceal her fury:

Carmel was the last absolute ruler at a time when the big advertisers were about to gain the upper hand. The times of the editor's unlimited power were coming to an end, TV was hard on the heels of the printed press and the hunt for lucrative advertising had begun. The major advertisers, who Carmel referred to scornfully as "the boys," even if they were very old, had precise needs. They wanted a say in the makeup and the illustration of the pages they paid for (handsomely). For Carmel this was unacceptable. It was up to her specialists alone to decide how to present a new brand of stockings or an old brand of tobacco. And the American advertisers always wanted, as the magazine was sold in America, to reach the American public. The Europe of which Carmel Snow was so fond left them indifferent. Yet in the battles that broke out around the editorial tables it was always Carmel's frail fist that hit the hardest. The advertisers themselves, the admen and the buyers, taken one by one, adored Carmel, following her advice to the letter. We owe a great deal of the favor won by Italy in America to her influence on the buyers.[30]

All this shed light on an editorial approach from which the Italy of
the fashion magazines still had a great deal to learn. The emerging
professional figures of the young Italian fashion publishing industry
regarded Carmel Snow as a model: a model who would show them
how to develop a correct professional code of conduct. I am reminded,
for example, of an article published in 1964 in which Irene Brin
wondered how to limit the negative effects on Italian fashion of the
corporatist system of advertising, a true "Minotaur."[31] How to deal
with the powerful system of the advertising agencies that held the
"purse strings" of publishing groups that, in turn, owned the
women's weeklies with a high circulation? The solution she offered
was a complex one, but Irene Brin had no doubts about the fact that
only accurate and independent information on and promotion of
Italian fashion by the specialized press could contribute to presenting
the right image, by opposing the powerful interests of those who held
the monopoly over every paid advertisement in the pages of dailies,
weeklies and monthlies.

Rome had literally fallen head over heels in love with Carmel Snow,
with her well-groomed appearance, her courtesy and her sense of
perfectionism and duty.

It was Carmel who shaped the image of the woman journalist that we are now
familiar with, extremely elegant – as Matilde Serao never had been. Slender, with
white hair that turned violet or blue according to the whim of "Attilio" in Rome or
"Carita & Alexandre" in Paris, you felt like applauding her whenever she entered a
public place. Her little feet moved with such mysterious grace that you couldn't tell
in which direction she was heading, while in reality she already knew exactly where
she was going. She wore the ribbons of various honors proudly; she had flown into
Paris in 1944 at the height of battle of the Ardennes and immediately afterward to
London, pummeled by German V2s, on a dual mission of propaganda and love. In
her eulogy, her best friend Janet Flanner wrote: "She was a Balzac capable of
sympathy and compassion." Practically all the great figures owed her something.
From Baron de Meyer, whom she got to know when he was already old, to Huene,
Avedon and Hirsche. She gave work to all of them, just as she did to the theater
critic Kenneth Tynan and the novelist Carson McCullers at the beginning of their
careers.[32]

At the gala presentation of the Fontana collection Carmel Snow wore
a Balenciaga dress in black faille, but her red satin gloves were Italian

and bore the signature of D'Auria. Snow established curious ties of
affection with the Roman noblewomen present at the event. It was
like looking at a sort of *tableau vivant*. At Palazzo Costaguti, on the
occasion of the last bash in honor of the celebrities of fashion, the
members of the Roman nobility decided to dress in sumptuous and
precious costumes dug out of their family wardrobes (Donna Maria
Tosti di Valminuta, Vittoria Pecci, Pimpin Migliori, etc.). It was a
spectacle within the spectacle: it would have been truly ingenuous at
a time when the world of the Roman aristocracy was so audaciously
engaged in the promotion of Roman and soon international couture
as well – it suffices to think of Princess Giovanna Caracciolo, who
signed herself Carosa, of Princess Lola Giovannelli and Simonetta
Colonna di Cesarò – to interpret that particular parade without
taking its fictional tone into account. What they were doing was
courteously mimicking the attire of the historical character, as it was
presented at Cinecittà.
At bottom the dual combination of cinema and fashion and
aristocracy and fashion underlined what a profound and invasive
operation of fictionalization of social communication had been set in
motion in those years, in line with an ethics of consumption of which
we are perhaps reaching the conclusion today.
Irene Brin had anticipated the bitter-sour climax of this epilogue in
her last work, the unpublished *1952, L'Italia che esplode*. There she
imagined her 1952 self working on the editorial staff of a fashion
magazine in 1968, the year in which she was actually writing:

[...] the art directors of international publications regard Christmas as an enormous
personal advertising campaign. It is not unusual for cruel discourses to be heard at
high level editorial meetings: "I've a great idea for December 1968. The lepers of the
island of Kanai. Cheap and lucrative. The Hawaiian tourist industry will put us up
and pay us a considerable sum. Timing. We can go there in March, that is before
going to Bolivia to collect the material for the Easter 1969 issue: the butchered Che
lives on in people's hearts... Well the lepers of Kanai are not contagious and love to
put on a performance. The only problem is that they are quickly cured and the
Americans even do plastic surgery on them. ... Better to bring it forward a month.
Shall we cover the carpet with a sheet of paper? My pointer, please. Look out... So.
Here, on the right, a group of ugly leper women, old and tragic. Very torn drapery:
lava gray, red-violet, at least one yellow. Sticks, crutches, all the necessary in short.
On the left the pretty lepers. Scanty clothing, if one of them has a breast missing,

photograph her from the other side. All in white, opaque. There could be a few little garlands, a dove clutched to the heart... Make sure that the heart is under the healthy breast. In the background at the center, the men of the tribe, with spears. Who said that the Hawaiians are peaceful and don't use spears? Nonsense Miss Furness. We'll borrow the spears from the Honolulu Museum or bring them with us from California. In the foreground the Madonna. Beautiful. At the most a little spot on the forehead... A halo of white flowers. Blue dress, and since she's squatting on the ground, be careful with the folds of the blue dress. Fifteenth-century Florentine. Next to her, St. Joseph. In a very bad state, very. Maimed? No, then he couldn't be a carpenter. One-eyed. A bandage over the eye. Everything clear so far? Signorina Myrtles, be careful with that bandage over St. Joseph's eye, it must *not* look like an advert for Hathaway shirts. In the middle, the Child. He should be a bit leprous too. And remember that we are collaborating indirectly with the charities, Corfam or whatever you prefer, *sending half a dollar a month you'll be supporting half a leper*... Essential detail: the child is lying with some leaves and grass in a wooden crate on which is written clearly, 'Eat Tropical Fruits.' Like the spears, you may have to bring the box with you from Los Angeles, I'm counting on you Miss Graves. This sheet should be reduced to a minimal scale, copied and subjected to the approval of the photographer, Mr. H.C. Brown. (In such cases the art director should arrange for a photographer of little importance, who'll follow orders and doesn't throw fits.) Thank you, ladies and gentlemen, for your energetic and stimulating participation."[33]

The accelerated pace of production and the requirements of the entertainment world had invaded fashion, stripping it of that ethical sense, that cultural commitment which, while aware of the "superficial" nature of the medium, Irene Brin had cherished over the long course of her career as a journalist. No longer present in the work she did for fashion was that sense of conquest of reality on the part of a young art, still capable of marveling at the world. In the passage quoted we find a form of that "abuse of the visual world"[34] that for Guy Debord was the product of the techniques of massive diffusion of images. Fashion here is not just a "malign muse," but a figure sterilely withdrawn into itself, characterized by a troubling self-referentiality.

Her experience had been a very different one when, in December 1951, *Harper's Bazaar* had entrusted her with the task of helping Henri Cartier-Bresson find the right setting for a photographic service to be published in the magazine the Christmas of the following year. By the way, it is worth noting that the lapse of time between the realization of the service and its publication in the magazine underlines the somewhat improvised character of this way of working: Christmas was not re-created artificially in the studio, but shot from life. It had been Marie-Louise Bousquet, the Paris editor of *Harper's Bazaar*, who had invited her to find "*un petit amour de petit Noël italien*."[35] She did her best to satisfy her, but the search proved an arduous one. From Naples, her friend Paolo Barbieri let her know that the city had more familiarity with thorns than with sweetmeats: Easter with its magnificent processions in black and purple was more in keeping with the spirit of the Parthenopean capital, more inclined to celebrate death than life. Then she had the idea to ask Donna Margherita Caetani for permission to photograph the seven half-ruined churches on her Ninfa estate, but Cartier-Bresson found the scene too D'Annunzian. Next it was the turn of a monsignor who was ready to let them take pictures of Mass in an enclosed convent, but the photographer thought this too baroque. All that was left was photographing the interminable line of devotees climbing and descending the steps of the Ara Coeli from the window of Palazzo Pecci-Blunt, but this proposal was rejected as well: "too Image d'Epinal or holy picture."[36] The quest seemed to be going nowhere when,

pursuing the image of a country that had perhaps ceased to exist, Eli and Henri spent December 1951 between Scanno and Matera. Communications were cut off, the snowplows weren't working and we corresponded thanks to the goodwill of Cesareo, Tamburri, the "poste restante" and the sellers of ricotta who brought me news of them: "Even though my wife is suffering a lot from the cold, we are happy that the people offer us a hospitality which must date back to ancient times." On three occasions that winter the Cartier-Bressons went to the South of Italy and climbed up to the Albergo d'Inghilterra, always bringing back excellent pictures.[37]

The living crèche at Scanno was judged perfect: the feature would be published in the December issue of the following year under the title "Christmas in Scanno."
It is unlikely today that a fashion feature would be prepared a year in advance, and the thought that in that theatricalized reality the possibility could be contemplated that life, even just that of fashion, would suspend all its unpredictability for such a long interval of time has the charm of a lost world. Regularly at Christmas *Harper's Bazaar*

would present the iconography of an archaic time, still possible to track down in more or less remote corners of the earth, evoking it to its readers in the illusion of being able to coincide with the time and the place of its last "presentification." The interval of a year between the time of the realization of the reportage and the consumption of the images was completely overshadowed.

When putting together a fashion reportage, it was the moment of construction of the illusion on which Irene Brin focused: the search for locations and the evocative power they provided. The journalist concentrated on the long series of shots that, in the dyschrony of gestures and words, would allow her to delineate the profile of the personalities involved and bring out their sensibility. The mesh of synergies and mutual cultural reverberations at work in the construction of the event, the garment or the accessory had to be grasped before they were fixed in the infinite allure of their appearance. And in a similar way what attracted her in the world of couture was the conception of a new fashion, something which always took place out of season, as Dior stressed in his autobiography: "Work is always done on the winter collection when the lilacs and cherries are in bloom. [...] The couturier is not a landscape painter of the Barbizon School: he does not work on what he sees in front of him; rather his creation comes closer to poetic expression. He needs a certain yearning."[38]

Irene Brin would not have renounced the mysterious quality of fashion, of the way that it is a medium between the media, and it was for this reason that she had never felt akin to the militant journalist, to the "passionate reporter" fanatic about every new style: "I am not excessively fond of columnists. But if I have to give them a suggestion, it will always be what was precious to me, in any period of collections: you have to try to understand fashion through the theater, books, museums."[39]

She would have appealed to the different dimensions of art not just because they were disciplines allied to fashion, its fields of application or sources of inspiration, but because together with fashion those disciplines contribute, in a continuous and fluid dissemination of the forms of expression, to amplifying the imaginative potential of the consumer of fashions. The spectral dimension of the "object" would

have fueled the continual bringing into play of illusion, a condition
necessary to the renewal of the entire fashion system:

> [...] among the little girls who mourned the poor Lucky in Saint Pierre de Chaillot,
> there was someone capable of taking up the scepter of Madame Rose Bertin, Marie-
> Antoinette's dressmaker, who survived her queen, her revolution, her poverty.
> Fashion, as we know very well, never dies,[40]

wrote Irene Brin in 1963 on the occasion of the death of Lucky
Daouphars, president and founder of the Parisian Association
Mutuelle des Mannequins. And it is suggestive, in further dyschrony,
to imagine that she wrote those words in the guise of a born-again
Madame Pompadour, a person to whom she had already been
compared, in November 1951, in the pages of *Harper's Bazaar*. For
those pages, her friend the photographer Karen Radkai had taken a
picture that serves as an interpretation all by itself. With the
inseparable pearls around her neck – perhaps a homage to Chanel –
the writer was shown in the position she habitually did her writing,
in her case on a typewriter: that is to say lying down, with her
shoulders propped against the head of her fine baroque bed, adorned
with spiral columns and cherubs as custodians of her inspiration.

NOTE_____

[1] Elsa Robiola, "America insegna," in *Bellezza*, no. 11 (1956),
p. 54.
[2] *Ibid.*
[3] Irene Brin, "Belle donne in serie, abiti belli in serie, ecco la formula della moda americana," in
*Bellezza*, no. 9 (1950), pp. 53-5.
[4] *Ibid.*
[5] Irene Brin, *Fanno loro la vera moda*, article written in 1949 for an unidentified periodical, now
in the Irene Brin Archives at the cultural association La Centrale dell'Arte.
[6] *Ibid.*
[7] *Ibid.*
[8] Emilio Cecchi, *America amara* (1939). Padua: Franco Muzzio Editore, 1995, p. 196.
[9] *Ibid.*
[10] Irene Brin, *Usi e Costumi 1920-1940*. Rome: Donatello De Luigi, 1944, p. 35.
[11] Irene Brin, "Obiettivi puntati sull'Italia," in *Bellezza*, no. 5 (1950), pp. 72-4.
[12] *Ibid.*
[13] *Ibid.*
[14] Irene Brin, "Best Sellers," in *Bellezza*, no. 10 (1959), p. 94.
[15] Irene Brin, "Sole d'Italia in pieno inverno di Nuova York,"
in *Bellezza*, no. 2 (1952), pp. 32-5.
[16] *Ibid.*

[17] *Ibid.*
[18] *Ibid.*
[19] Irene Brin, "Con le attrici italiane a Nuova York," in *Bellezza*, no. 12 (1952), p. 62.
[20] *Ibid.*
[21] *Ibid.*
[22] *Ibid.*
[23] Nina Borghese, "Italy," in *Time*, January 29, 1965.
[24] Germano Celant, *Roma - New York 1948-1964*. Milan: Charta, 1993, pp. 21-2.
[25] Ivi, pp. 82-5.
[26] *Ibid.*
[27] *Ibid.*
[28] Irene Brin, *1952, L'Italia che esplode*, [unpublished], quoted from the typescript, p. 26.
[29] Ivi, p. 21.
[30] Ivi, p. 22.
[31] Irene Brin, "Affrontiamo il Minotauro della moda,"
in *Bellezza*, no. 6 (1964), p. 96.
[32] Irene Brin, *1952, L'Italia che esplode*, [unpublished], quoted from the typescript, p. 23.
[33] Ivi, p. 9.
[34] Guy Debord, *La Société du spectacle* (1975); Engl. ed. *The Society of the Spectacle*, trans. by Donald Nicholson-Smith. New York: Zone Books, 1994.
[35] Irene Brin, *1952, L'italia che esplode*, [unpublished], quoted from the typescript, pp. 11-2.
[36] *Ibid.*
[37] *Ibid.*
[38] Christian Dior, "Christian Dior et moi," in P. Colaiacomo, V.C. Caratozzolo (eds.), *Mercante di stile*. Rome: Editori Riuniti, 2002, p. 169.
[39] Irene Brin, "Capire Parigi," in *Bellezza*, no. 3 (1957), p. 84.
[40] Irene Brin, "La moda non muore mai," in *Bellezza*, no. 9 (1963), p. 69.

THINGS I SAW

Irene Brin's bookplate, from her collection of *Harper's Bazaar*. Courtesy Accademia di Costume e di Moda, Rome

Drawing by Bruno Caruso for the cover of Irene Brin's
book *Usi e costumi 1920-1940*. Courtesy Fondi Storici,
Galleria Nazionale d'Arte Moderna, Rome

Cover of *Usi e Costumi 1920-1940*

Newspaper cutting of Jean Harlow made by Irene
Brin. Courtesy Archivio Irene Brin, La Centrale
dell'Arte

Chirico

Lepri

Music

Vespignani

Caruso

Cagli

Pagliacci

Colombotto Rosso

Berman

Piletti

Clerici

## LA GALLERIA DELL'OBELISCO

DI

### *Irene Brin*

in *Via Sistina 146 a Roma*

raccoglie ed espone i libri e le cose più belle di tutti i secoli. Così il presente talvolta si sovrappone al passato o viceversa. Nella foto che pubblichiamo qui accanto, è appunto un modello di Carosa che si appoggia su preziosissimi ninnoli e su minime stampe del migliore Rinascimento Italiano e straniero.

## RATTO D'EUROPA DI PAOLO VERONESE

Un dettaglio del « Ratto di Europa » di Paolo Veronese ha suggerito questo armonioso vestito da sera.

Il serico broccato che riappare in molte collezioni di alta moda non conferisce nulla di arcaico alla creazione. Anche la forma della scollatura, largamente quadrata, è di piena attualità. Non c'è nulla da trasportare o da sostituire all'originale del capolavoro. Il bustino a punta, la gala di merletto, l'acconciatura e i gioielli s'intonano perfettamente al gusto di oggi.

Il décolleté che può sembrare un tantino eccessivo varrà indubbiamente a dimostrare che le deprecate scollature moderne peccano, se mai, solamente di modestia.

(disegno di GIONGUIDA).

Publicity for the Galleria L'Obelisco, Rome, photo by Pasquale De Antonis. From *Orchidea*, January 1947. Courtesy Fondi Storici, Galleria Nazionale d'Arte Moderna, Rome

Illustrations of the obelisk. From Graham Greene, Lionello Venturi, André Breton (eds.), *L'Obelisco*, Rome 1955. Courtesy Fondi Storici, Galleria Nazionale d'Arte Moderna, Rome

Irene Brin with the obelisk, photo by Leslie Gill. Courtesy
Fondi Storici, Galleria Nazionale d'Arte Moderna, Rome

Irene Brin and Gaspero del Corso in the Galleria L'Obelisco,
photo by Leslie Gill, 1947. The book is *La Gerusalemme liberata*,
illustrated with etchings by Piazzetta in 1745. Courtesy Fondi
Storici, Galleria Nazionale d'Arte Moderna, Rome

# UN ALTRO OBELISCO

*a Roma*

Carosa dress, photo by Pasquale De Antonis.
From "Un altro obelisco a Roma," in *Bellezza*, yr. II,
no. 12-13, December 1946. Courtesy Accademia
di Costume e di Moda, Rome. Donated by Irene Brin

Carosa dress, photo by Pasquale De Antonis.
From "Un altro obelisco a Roma," in *Bellezza*, yr. II,
no. 12-13, December 1946. Courtesy Archivio De
Antonis, Rome

Leonor Fini, *Portrait of Princess Francesca Blanc Ruspoli*, photo by Ghergo. From Irene Brin,
"Entusiasmi," in *Bellezza*, yr. IV, no. 29, March-April 1948. Courtesy Accademia
di Costume e di Moda, Rome. Donated by Irene Brin.
"Is this a human being or a fashion plate? – some candid critics ask about Leonor's society
portraits." (From Mario Praz, "Leonor Fini: Gothic Painter," in *View*, vol. VII, 1946)

Irene Brin, photo by Pasquale De Antonis, 1946. Courtesy Archivio De Antonis, Rome

# L'OBELISCO

MOSTRE TENUTE ALLA GALLERIA DELL'OBELISCO DAL NOVEMBRE 1946 AL LUGLIO 1955

1946 Morandi, Cristofanetti *, 1947 Vespignani, Carta, Bartolini, Tot, Lelia Caetani *, Scordia, Paresce, Toulouse Lautrec *, Mirko, Vagnetti, Campigli. 1948 de Chirico, Lorenzo Guerrini, Carlo Levi, Fasola, Tot, Pitture del primo periodo di de Pisis, de Chirico, Pirandello, Ferrazzi, Campigli, Francalancia; Pallavicini, Vespignani, Afro, Chiappelli, Cocteau *, Corrado Cagli, Titina Maselli *, Music, Pagliacci *, Dalì *, Rosina Viva, Leda Mastrocinque. 1949 de Chirico, M. G. Dal Monte, Agnes Muthspiel *, Carlo Quaglia, Arrigo Episcopi, Marino Marini, Ercolani, Bargheer, Fabrizio Clerici, « Portonaccio »: Vespignani, Muccini, Urbinati; Savinio e Samminiatelli, Eugène Berman *, Della Torre, Tallone, Renato Galleani, Corot, Harvey Fite *, Herbert List *, Tamburi, Salvador *, Gio Ponti, Gioielli di Masenza *, Ceramiche di Val D'Inferno *. 1950 Matta *, Rosita Tacconi, Giovanni Fattori, Golovin *, Alberto Tavazzi, Stanislao Lepri, Eugenio Dragutesco, de Chirico, Carlo Quaglia, Aldo Pagliacci, Pavel Tchelitchew *, Antonio Music, Pic *, Michael Ayrton *, Sebastiano Carta, Corrado Cagli, Ildebrando Urbani, Carlo Farkas *, Nino Caffè, Seurat, Orologi Francesi '700 e '800, Enrico Donati, Piccole sculture di Macrì, Letizia Cerio, Antonio Corpora, Gauguin, Fabio Rieti e Gilles Aillaud *. 1951 Monsù Desiderio *, Kandinsky, Zuccheri, Marcello Muccini *, Stanley Brandon Kearl *, Leda Mastrocinque, Manlio Helfrich Guberti, Barbasetti di Prun *, Hans Jenny *, Titina De Filippo, Ludovisi, De Antonis *, Minei, Greenberg *, Saul Steinberg *, Pagliacci, de Regibus *, Die Hundsgruppe *, Nino Caffè, Utamaro e Modigliani, Music, 5 pavimenti di Capogrossi, Clavè *, « Danza, Circo e Music Hall ». 1952 Burri, R. M. de Angelis, « Viaggio in Italia », Carlo Fontana, Corrado Cagli, Bernard Childs *, Franco Marzotto, Ruggero Michaelles, Enrico Accatino, Mirko, Mario Russo, Pagliacci, Giordano Falzoni *, George Biddle *, Marc Chagall, Lyda de Francisci, Käthe Kollwitz *, Carlo Quaglia, « I gatti ». 1953 Assenza, Campigli Grafico, Magritte *, Berardinone *, Rosai, Tanguy *, Antonio Calderara, Scatole e Feticci di Bob Rauschenberg *, Kay Sage *, Franco Gentilini, « Immagini Bizantine » *, Ivan Mosca, Colombotto Rosso *, Hedda Sterne *, Bruno Caruso *, Afro, Picasso: « Chef d'oeuvre inconnu », Fabius Gugel *, Renzo Vespignani, Giuditta Scalini, Linda Chittaro *, Arte Maya *, Carlo Guarienti, Enzo Frascione, L'America immaginata da 20 pittori italiani, Enotrio *, Sironi, Gertrude Schweitzer, William Congdon *, Zao Wou-Ki *, « L'amore ». 1954 Enrico d'Assia *, Fatti del giorno, Hans Erni *, Vertès *, Martin de Alzaga *, I Picasso di Mosca *, Guglielmo Emanuel, Gentilini, Pagliacci, Léonid *, Burri, Bruno Caruso, Maria Savinio *, Emilio Greco, Antero Piletti *, Music, Mirò, Nino Caffè, Carlyle Brown *, Leonardo Cremonini, « Joie de vivre ». 1955 Marcello Avenali, Hector Escobosa *, 5 pittori - 5 scultori, Bernard Buffet *, Tchelitchew, Zuccheri, Vera Strawinsky *, Roberto Fasola, I « tre P », Clavè e Maria Sanmartì, Mario Russo, Marcello Muccini, Antonio Camarca *, Renzo Vespignani, Ivan Mosca. (* Per la prima volta in Italia)

List of the artists who had shown at the Galleria
L'Obelisco. From Graham Greene, Lionello Venturi,
André Breton (eds.), *L'Obelisco*, Rome 1955. Courtesy
Fondi Storici, Galleria Nazionale d'Arte Moderna,
Rome

Cover of the catalogue *L'Obelisco*. From Graham Greene, Lionello
Venturi, André Breton (eds.), *L'Obelisco*, Rome 1955. Courtesy Fondi
Storici, Galleria Nazionale d'Arte Moderna, Rome

*following pages*
"Imaginary Views of America by Italian Painters." From *Vogue*,
October 15, 1953

# IMAGINARY VIEWS OF AMERICA
## BY ITALIAN PAINTERS

**FRANCO GENTILINI, "BROOKLYN BRIDGE"**

Gentilini, the first painter asked to paint his idea of America (where he had never been), chose the Brooklyn Bridge, because "It has grandeur and romance . . . and is always being sold."

**IVAN MOSCA, "MISSISSIPPI DELTA"**

Mosca, a painter with an extraordinarily rich colour sense, is also a student of entomology. Into his imaginary view of the great river's mouth, he put three hitherto unheard-of species of box-like butterflies.

**NINO CAFFÈ, "BASEBALL"**

Caffè's enchanting baseball game involves not only the usual eighteen players, but an energetic group of priests, introduced because Caffè enjoys painting them. (At forty-five, he is the senior artist in this group.)

**BRUNO CARUSO, "ICE CREAM VENDOR IN BROOKLYN"**

Caruso said of his ice cream man, "[He] is an immigrant . . . just arrived. It is winter. He was informed that America was warm. . . . Naturally, he is sad."

**GIORDANO FALZONI, "LOUISIANA BAYOU"**

Falzoni, twenty-six years old, paints a mysterious bayou peopled with skeletons of plants and animals, overhung by an oil well, and wonderfully miasmal.

These views of America, painted by Italian artists who have never seen America, are among twenty commissioned in Rome, last spring, by Princess Gourielli—internationally known as Helena Rubinstein. A connoisseur of painting, and protean collector, Mme. Rubinstein was charmed by the freshness, vitality, and technical skill of the young Italian painters whose work she saw; was so struck by their interest in America that she asked twenty of them to paint their ideas of what it looked like. In June, the twenty canvases (plus thirty drawings) were exhibited in Rome; then, at the request of the Italian Government, in Capri. Starting October fifteenth, they will be shown at Mme. Rubinstein's own gallery in New York for the benefit of the Hospitalized Veterans Music Service, then will tour American museums—giving American viewers an oddly provocative glimpse of their own country. (Perhaps, somewhere in Brooklyn, there really *is* an ice cream man wearing a harlequin collar.)

ANTONIO MUSIC, "INDIAN AMERICA"

Music, a leading Italian painter, has never visited the U.S., although many of his works are here (some in the Museum of Modern Art). His vision of the Great Plains is like a primitive wall-painting.

AFRO, "CHICAGO"

Afro, who lives and works in Rome, sees Chicago as a mass of violent, plunging verticals. He has had one-man shows in America; is represented in such collections as the Barnes Foundation in Merion, Pa.

COLOMBOTTO ROSSO,
"THE ROCKY MOUNTAINS"

Rosso, young and whimsical, paints the Rockies emerging from a moonlit sea, with allegorical figures. His work reminds some people of Dürer, some of Chinese art, some of William Blake.

ALBERTO BURRI, "JAZZ"

Burri, considered "the most disconcerting of all Italian abstractionists," gave this as his idea of America: Jazz, represented by blobs of colour on gold. Once a doctor, he renounced medicine to do his effective paintings.

*On page 116, more about four painters in this group.*

Schuberth dress, illustration by Federico Pallavacini.
From Irene Brin, "Corriere da Roma," in *Bellezza*, yr. VI, no. 15,
February 1947. Courtesy Accademia di Costume e di Moda, Rome.
Donated by Irene Brin

Fontana dresses, Galleria L'Obelisco, photo by Pasquale De Antonis.
From "*Bellezza*," no. 24-25, 1947. Courtesy Accademia di Costume
e di Moda, Rome. Donated by Irene Brin

A concentrare
maggiormente l'interesse
sulla "guêpière"
un ricamo in perline
orna la parte liscia
di quest'abito da pranzo
ricco di pieghe sciolte
nella gonna,
morbido anche
fra spalle e seno.
Paravento
di Renzo Vespignani.

Un corpetto
di raso bianco
punteggiato di jais
e disseminato
di fiori ricamati in nero,
rischiara
questo abito in velluto
da mezza sera,
scollato,
ma a spalle coperte.
Gioielli di Luciana.
Paravento di Cristofanetti.

*FONTANA*

*FONTANA*

*fotografie De Antonis alla Galleria dell'Obelisco*

Clelia Venturi hats, photos by Pasquale De Antonis.
From "Alla Toulouse Lautrec," in *Bellezza*, yr. III,
no. 18-19, 1947. Courtesy Accademia di Costume
e di Moda, Rome. Donated by Irene Brin

TOULOUSE LAUTREC (OBELISCO 1947)

TOULOUSE FA IL RITRATTO A LAUTREC MONFÀ

A FIANCO: COPERTINA DI RENZO VESPIGNANI
PER LA MOSTRA LAUTREC (OBELISCO 1947)

"Alla Toulouse Lautrec," photo by Pasquale De Antonis. From *Bellezza*,
yr. III, no. 18-19, 1947. Courtesy Accademia di Costume
e di Moda, Rome. Donated by Irene Brin

Toulouse Lautrec, Galleria L'Obelisco, 1947. Cover by Renzo Vespignani.
From Graham Greene, Lionello Venturi, André Breton (eds.), *L'Obelisco*,
Rome 1955. Courtesy Fondi Storici, Galleria Nazionale d'Arte Moderna,
Rome

Ever since the opening of the Galleria L'Obelisco, Irene Brin had been conscious of how important it was that any sort of cultural activity should get immediate coverage in the media; a general rule that was of great help to her in the promotion of her own work and in obtaining the funding she needed to put on exhibitions of art and fashion shows: "In 1952 I received a letter from a millionaire in Punta del Este that went more or less as follows: "At my nightclub I could organize a festival of Italian fashion or a striptease show by French girls. I know that you dress well, would you organize the fashion show for me? I'll pay for everything, the journey out, the mannequins, the journey back." I replied that I would accept only if he put on, again at his expense, a completely different exhibition in Montevideo: *Jovines y Maestros en la Pintura Italiana de Hoy*. He agreed, so long as I would speak every evening on one of the many radio stations he controlled. Along with the creations of Italian fashion, works by Modigliani, de Chirico, Severini and Burri set off for South America. And so, every evening, I advised Uruguayans to season their salads with a certain oil produced by our patron. I got very good at it." The episode marked the beginning of a long series of exhibitions staged abroad: however, it was no longer manufacturers of oil who invited Irene Brin, but directors of major American museums.

(From an interview given by Irene Brin and Gaspero del Corso to the magazine *Domus*, in *Domus*, no. 403, June 1963)

"I successi italiani nel mondo," publicity for the Galleria
L'Obelisco, drawing by Brunetta. From *Bellezza*, yr. XVI,
no. 7, July 1956. Courtesy Accademia di Costume
e di Moda, Rome. Donated by Irene Brin

Anche la pittura moderna italiana sta brillantemente avviandosi a prendere nel quadro internazionale delle arti il posto che merita. A cura della Galleria dell'Obelisco di Roma alcune città degli Stati Uniti fra le quali Cincinnati, San Francisco, New Orleans e New York hanno di recente ospitato una Mostra di quadri di autori italiani di tendenze diverse: dalle firme già famose a quelle dei giovani di oggi. Da sinistra, Irene Brin, comproprietaria della Galleria, a destra, contro la parete, Gaspare Dal Corso che ne è il dinamico Direttore. Il disegno è dovuto al pennello di Brunetta.

# i successi italiani nel mondo

Le tradizioni di buon gusto ed eleganza del nostro popolo che hanno dato all'arte, all'artigianato e all'industria italiana i più lusinghieri consensi in tutto il mondo, hanno trovato conferma nel successo del Tabacco d'Harar, il profumo italiano venduto a Londra, a Parigi, a New York, a Stoccolma, a Berlino, a Vienna ancor più che in Italia. La tonalità originale e la caratteristica confezione del Tabacco d'Harar hanno riscosso il favore della signora e dell'uomo eleganti e raffinati d'ogni paese. È il profumo dalla nota singolare che assume particolari sfumature in ogni clima e su ogni persona, sempre uguale e sempre nuovo.

## Profumo e Colonia
# TABACCO D'HARAR

Anna Magnani in the "La voce umana" episode of *L'amore*, directed
by Roberto Rossellini, 1948. From Matilde Hochkofler, *Anna Magnani*,
Rome 1984

foto Dormer

**LEONOR FINI** *riposa, o finge di riposare, in un* *balletto ai "Champs Elysées" ancora con scenari e costumi*
*meditatissimo atteggiamento e in una nuvola di pizzi, piume,* *suoi, musica di Gretry, coreografia di Roland Petit. Al*
*taffetà attraentissale. E compiono un attimo di sosta nella* *Metropolitan di New York, durante quest'inverno, che la*

Leonor Fini, photo by Dormer. From *Bellezza*,
yr. III, no. 23, 1947. Courtesy Accademia di Costume
e di Moda, Rome. Donated by Irene Brin

*L'ultima trovata delle esistenzialiste romane*, mid-fifties. © Longanesi
& C. Photo by Mercurio Milano. Courtesy Fondi Storici, Galleria
Nazionale d'Arte Moderna, Rome

Irene Brin, photo by Karen Radkai. From *Harper's Bazaar*,
November 1951

Salvador Dalí, *Portrait of Helena Rubinstein*, 1942-43. From Suzanne Slesin, *Over the Top. Helena Rubinstein: Extraordinary Style*. New York: Pointed Leaf Press, 2003.
"The old myth of mutability and interpretation has found a new example in Helena Rubinstein, Princess Gourielli. This woman faithful to herself, loyal to her friends, stubborn in her arbitrarily chosen tasks and her freely accepted duties, likes to see herself through other people's eyes and has asked to have her portrait painted by Salvador Dalí and Raoul Dufy, Marie Laurencin and Candido Portinari, Corrado Cagli and Pavlick Tchelitcheff. I've mentioned six of them, and left out another sixty. In her aerial house in New York, in her flying house in Paris, in her villa in Provence, earthbound instead and held down by trees, Helena Rubinstein can continually look at her reflection in canvases that each reveal a different woman."
(From *Una Centomila Tutte*, early 1950s, published in an unidentified periodical, Archivio Irene Brin, Associazione Culturale La Centrale dell'Arte)

Irene Brin, photo by Ghergo

Cover by Salvador Dalí for William Shakespeare,
*As You Like It*, in the version staged by the
Compagnia Italiana di Prosa, directed by Luchino
Visconti. Rome: Carlo Bestetti Edizioni d'Arte, 1948.
Courtesy Archivio Fabrizio Clerici, Rome

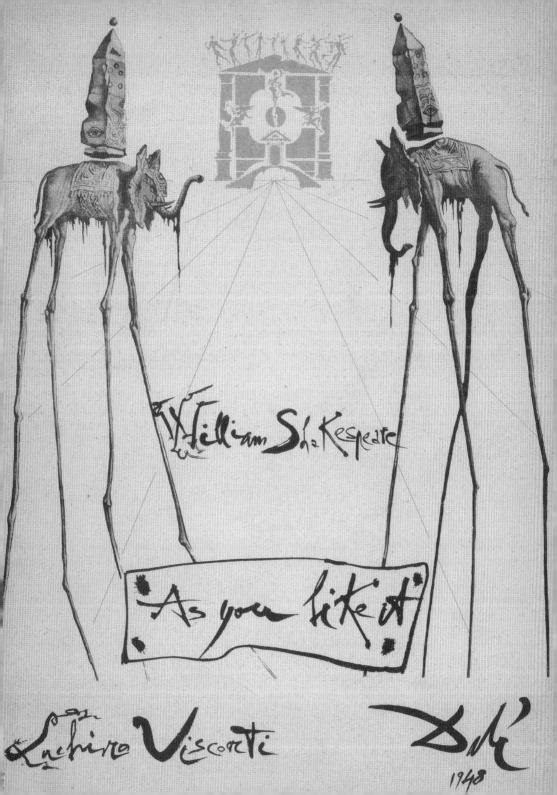

William Shakespeare

As you like it

Luchino Visconti                    Dalí
                                    1948

VAINCUR

Dali
1948

JANVIER

Fontana dress, photo by Pasquale De Antonis. From "Salvador Dalí in sartoria,"
in *Bellezza*, yr. IX, no. 1, January 1949. Courtesy Accademia di Costume e di Moda,
Rome. Donated by Irene Brin

Salvador Dalí, sketches of Vaneur and Olivier's costumes for Shakespeare's
*As You Like It*, directed by Luchino Visconti, Teatro Eliseo, November 26, 1948.
From William Shakespeare, *As You Like It*, in the version staged by the Compagnia
Italiana di Prosa, directed by Luchino Visconti. Rome: Carlo Bestetti Edizioni
d'Arte, 1948. Courtesy Archivio Fabrizio Clerici, Rome

Scenery for Shakespeare's *As You Like It*, directed by
Luchino Visconti, Teatro Eliseo, November 26, 1948.
From *Venti spettacoli di Luchino Visconti*, ed. by Mario
Ramous. Bologna 1958

Vivi Gioi, Rina Morelli e Vittorio Gassman in Rosalinda o Come vi piace di Shakespeare, regia di Luchino Visconti (19-

Vivi Gioi, Rina Morelli eVittorio Gassman in Shakespeare's
*As You Like It*, directed by Luchino Visconti, Teatro Eliseo,
November 26, 1948. From Maurizio Giammuso, *Eliseo.
Un teatro e i suoi protagonisti*, Rome 1989

Paolo Stoppa, Rina Morelli and Vivi Gioi in Shakespeare's *As You Like It*, directed by Luchino Visconti, Teatro Eliseo, November 26, 1948. From Maurizio Fagiolo dell'Arco, Claudia Terenzi (eds.), *Roma 1948-1959*, Milan: Skira, 2002

Salvador Dalí, sketches of Rosalind and Celia's costumes for Shakespeare's *As You Like It*, directed by Luchino Visconti, Teatro Eliseo, November 26, 1948. From William Shakespeare, *As You Like It*, in the version staged by the Compagnia Italiana di Prosa, directed by Luchino Visconti. Rome: Carlo Bestetti Edizioni d'Arte, 1948. Courtesy Archivio Fabrizio Clerici, Rome

Palmer dress, photo by Pasquale De Antonis. From "Salvador Dalí in sartoria," in *Bellezza*, yr. IX, no. 1, January 1949. Courtesy Accademia di Costume e di Moda, Rome. Donated by Irene Brin.
"[…] My costumes are morphological and, to serve my audience better, prophetic too. They are not, in fact, simply 18th-century clothes, but clothes that were on the point of being realized, of taking on substance. Clothes that threatened to become just that, clothes that, in ten years, pretty much all of us will be wearing." (From Salvador Dalí, "Bonjour," in William Shakespeare *As You Like It*, in the version staged by the Compagnia Italiana di Prosa, directed by Luchino Visconti. Rome: Carlo Bestetti Edizioni d'Arte, 1948)

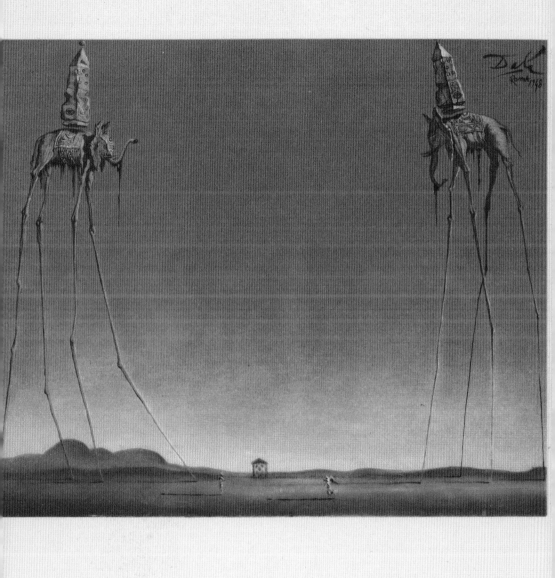

Scenery by Salvador Dalí for Shakespeare's *As You Like It*, directed by Luchino Visconti.
Teatro Eliseo, November 26, 1948. From William Shakespeare, *As You Like It*, in the
version staged by the Compagnia Italiana di Prosa, directed by Luchino Visconti. Rome:
Carlo Bestetti Edizioni d'Arte, 1948. Courtesy Archivio Fabrizio Clerici, Rome

Luciana De Reutern
questa grande collana
di sua creazione con
chini e braccialetti as

# il Nord e il Sud

Rinnegando ogni evocazione di crinoline e di gale offerte dal Nord e dal Sud di "Via col Vento" il nostro Sud in vuole piatte ed le strade costellate di macerie. Un Sud modesto, ma benario, un Nord modesto, ma orgoglioso e le donne discese appena dal camion impolverati confrontano due mode indipendenti fino al separatismo, convalidate dalle testimonianze della rivista di moda americana giunta a Roma e della rivista di moda francese giunta a Torino. A quest'esile traccia ci affidiamo le Romane per affermare il gran riccolo curvato che copre loro la fronte, l'assenza assoluta di maniche, la gonna lunghetta a Santa Margherita scopre gli scialletti di lana d'Angora bianca, l'abitino corto di merletto bianco con cintura cremisi e fuccia [zandalini assortiti] e se ne adorna a casa sua. I sandali d'oro, trinati fermi da una stella che pone tra pollice e indice non solo una elaborata di passo, ma anche un segno indubbiamente marino e celeste, dilagano di Via Condotti verso Via Montenapoleone incrociandosi con gli ombrelli altissimi, infocchettati sul manico, allargati da una balza intorno alla cupola, perfetti per il solo, oppure rigidamente impermeabilizzati e pronti ad invadere Roma. Piccoli giochi di gente povera, ma garbata, invenzioni per donne coraggiose, ma incrinate dal rammarico: "Ho ventidue anni", sospira Elisabetta, "un marito, due figli ed ancora non ho mai portato un vestito lungo, non sono mai stata ad un vero ballo!". E Cristina: "Ho trentanuno e devo adottare il motto di mia nonna che ne aveva settanta, à notre âge, mon enfant, on ne s'habille pas, on se couvre!". E ciascuna candidamente spera che del territori ancora difficilmente raggiungibili, misteriosi secondo un computo di chilometri e di gomme bucate, le giunga almeno la possibilità di uno scambio: chi porrà nello Harry's Bar di Venezia la lapide [in cera stampata] testimoniante un incontro quasi storico, una Fiera delle Vanità mutata fino ad essere commovente? Non si conoscevano affatto. La donna del Sud stava davanti al bancone con l'abito in jersey artificialissimo, già rammendato nelle scannellature del drappeggi, la donna del Nord ne nacchetti: le cornice del resto sembrava immutata, gli uomini non tanto giovani che traggono la loro eleganza da una sciarpa gialla e dava'aria di solenne stolidità discorrevano con Cipriani, le donne non tanto giovani che affidano la loro seduzione al lineamento eretto, al far maligno di chi ha vissuto un tempo sofferono e se ne vevono ora di arena, perfezionando l'impostura del naso, il corruganti delle sopracciglia chiaccheravano martellanti e falsamente interessate con ragazzi senza importanza. Insomma l'aria era la stessa di sempre, un acquario sulle cui pareti di vetro erano

passati vanamente gli anni e le guerre rappresentate ora solo e con minezza dai ramificaleschi l jersey artificiale, dai mutamenti nel crespo a fiori e furono naturalmente le due eroine del dopoguerra a dar prove di un durevole entusiasmo nella frivolità quando la Nordica si alzò, curva verso la Meridionale, quasi affannata le chiese il segreto del suoi orecchini, glieli tolse, se li provò, tornando fiera al tavolo deve le amiche l'aspettavano, ad una ad una ornate del gioiello inatteso.

Era, inutile quasi a dirsi, un gioiello di Luciana. Spero che le donne non siano ingrate, e, disponendo domani di tessuti a miglia, di cappelli a staia, di acconari a tonnellate, rammentino di aver dovuto durante anni interi la loro fantasia e la loro grazia unicamente a queste donnesche meraviglie che al apparentano, sì, a Ninive e a Babilonia, poiché la baronessa de Reutern studia enormi volumi d'arte antica per trarne il fragile bottino di una sola buccola, ma sembrano soprattutto costituire un pronto soccorso di civetteria. Chi avrebbe salvato i millieuri, facilissimamente tratti dalle giubbe annesse dal marito, se non si fosse potuto appuntare sulla revuscia un solo d'oro, giustamente immesso e ripreso dall'altro docile intorno a polso? Il modo era grigio, il coprifuoco cominciava alle cinque, però dal lobo sinistro pendeva una lacrima verde, dal destro una lacrima rossa e non chiedete a noi il perché del capriccio. I nostri cappotti sapevano, tutti, di falso latte, di falsa lana, di falsa sicurezza, ma la borchia che li chiudeva intorno al colletto (uno di pelliccia, nessuno disponeva di pelliccia) era almeno lustra ed allegra. E se Giovanni Comisso riconosce in parecchie tra noi le condannate alla morte prossima, meravigliandosi per il rossetto sulle nostre labbra, per le belle pieghe nei capelli di Orsola, almeno il nostro di velluto stretto intorno al collo, illustrato da un grosso gruppo di strasse, ci rese simili alle amiche di Madame Tallien. Frecce, archi, turchesi, alì, olingi, mani, ucelli, leoni, obelischi, fiori, frutti, sirene, onvenerembi nelle curve del metallo dorate, sfolgoranti di vetri politi, ci offrirono le possibilità delle Mille e una Notte ed ora passando il mare le offriranno ad Americane ignare del clima di perseveranza e difficoltà cui le scoperte di Luciana devono probabilmente il loro insatte maggiore, appagate naturale da un satro anche per loro incosueto. Come scoopfecanmo il bottone raffigurante un sacchetto, con il milione di dollari dentro? Forse rammentando la vecchia canzone che ci ricondosce a Clara Bow, alle mistiche goldiggers: non diversamente la grande fibbia da cintura evoca fanciulle Parsoun, allo stesso modo aseltato d'oro e di civetterie e gli ornamenti in ceramica smaltata di mero, di rosso e di giallo suggeriscono misteri frangibili, un parnetsni. E difatti il meccanismo delle chiusure, perfino la disposizione dei grovigli presentano la riservatezza, la lieve difficoltà particolare agli oggetti costruiti su misura, dalle mani stesse dell'artigiano, estrema raffinatesa di

*(continuazione a fine fascicolo)*

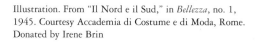

Illustration. From "Il Nord e il Sud," in *Bellezza*, no. 1, 1945. Courtesy Accademia di Costume e di Moda, Rome. Donated by Irene Brin

Cover of *Bellezza*, illustration by Leonor Fini, yr. I, no. 1, November 1945. Courtesy Accademia di Costume e di Moda, Rome. Donated by Irene Brin

Luciana De Reutern wearing jewelry of her own design, photo by Luxardo. From "Il Nord e il Sud," in *Bellezza*, no. 1, 1945. Courtesy Accademia di Costume e di Moda, Rome. Donated by Irene Brin

*following pages*
Frattegiani collection, 1946. From *Bellezza*, yr. II, no. 12-13, December 1946. Courtesy Accademia di Costume e di Moda, Rome. Donated by Irene Brin

dalla nuova collezione

FRATTE-
GIANI.

1 scarpa oro tutte
foglioline intorno
alla pianta

2 sandalo in fogli
di camosci multico

3 sandalo a lacci
lini tenuti da
fiocco in taffetè

4 sandalo raso n
tacco a ruola oro

5 scarpa camoscio vio
bowi oro.

6 sandalo lacci o
suola in paillet

di Frattegiani

FRAT

GIAN

1 stivaletto con rovescio di pelliccia.

2-3 stivaletti con tacco rotondo.

4 scarpa in camoscio nero.

5 scarpa con tacco rotondeggiante

6 scarpa camoscio marrone

7 scarpa vitello ma

8 pantofola gondola rosa oro

*CAROSA*

*Carosa propone l'abito estivo elegante, e per molte occasioni, in batista beige ricamata a punto inglese: cintura, cappello, guanti in taffetas nero. Sulla pagina opposta. Libri vede l'abito estivo da sera come lo sognano tutte le donne giovani e meno giovani: ricamo di San Gallo bianco, sottabito in taffetas scozzese, cintura del medesimo taffetas. Guanti a "mitaines" in San Gallo.*

# ESTATE A ROMA

Carosa dress, photo by Federico Pallavicini. From Irene Brin, "Estate a Roma," in *Bellezza*, no. 5, May 1949. Courtesy Accademia di Costume e di Moda, Rome. Donated by Irene Brin

Libri dress, photo by Federico Pallavicini. From Irene Brin, "Estate a Roma," in *Bellezza*, no. 5, May 1949. Courtesy Accademia di Costume e di Moda, Rome. Donated by Irene Brin

Schuberth dress, photo by Federico Pallavicini. From Irene Brin, "Estate a Roma," in *Bellezza*, no. 5, May 1949. Courtesy Accademia di Costume e di Moda, Rome. Donated by Irene Brin

And on the subject of hats, this is how Irene Brin recalled a day of shopping in Paris in 1952: "We bought, in the Vollard edition, Balzac's *Le chef d'oeuvre inconnu*, illustrated by Picasso with etchings that formed another exhibition for our winter. And then, seized with frivolity for a moment, I bought three hats to wear with the black skirt and jacket that, in Diana Vreeland's opinion, I would find indispensable during my stay in America.

"The first, yellow one, I bought in Place Vendôme, at a sale at Schiaparelli's: Schiaparelli was coming to the end of her gloriously inventive career; she had spent the war years in America, returning to her atelier after the end of hostilities. […] The second hat I bought almost by chance, passing through Rue Alfred de Vigny, where, at number 8, there was a small building in a neo-Romantic style and a sign with the word "soldes." In the best manner of the sale, in fact, the merchandise inside was piled on tables. Hats overflowed from baskets, and customers could pick them out and try them on by themselves. I chose a white hat, with a few black smudges on it: the young giant who appeared behind me smiled when he saw my uncertainty: "If you leave me your address, madam, I will get it cleaned for you." The smudges vanished and I went back innumerable times to the young giant, who had set up shop on Avenue Georges V. His name was Hubert de Givenchy.

"The third hat I saw at Balenciaga's, where, at that time, hats were still on display and not, as is the case today, just ancient statues and bottles of perfume. A wise precaution against thieves of ideas like me: in fact I went straight to the Galeries Lafayette to buy a tiny hat of black felt on which to pin a flat white camellia. It looked identical to Balenciaga's one. Now it seems absurd that three Parisian hats could give me such confidence and power. For me, they were three talismans."

(From Irene Brin, *1952, L'Italia che esplode*, [unpublished], pp. 78, 78 bis).

Ophelia hats, photo by Federico Pallavicini.
From Irene Brin, "Estate a Roma," in *Bellezza*,
no. 5, May 1949. Courtesy Accademia di Costume
e di Moda, Rome. Donated by Irene Brin

VELLUTO E PIQUÉ. Sopra: Calottina in velluto nero, ala mossa e irregolare in piqué bianco a nido d'ape, inamidato.

OPHELIA

FOGLIE E FIORI. Toque di foglioline verdi e gardenie bianche. Un pettine montato a gardenie può essere aggiunto all'acconciatura.

OPHELIA

MATASSA DI PAGLIA. Cappello in paglia nera. La paglia è usata come una matassa di filato e l'acconciatura si fonde con i capelli.

non può accompagnarci: verrà per qualche fine di settimana, per ferragosto. Gli uomini, sai!

Gli uomini si trasformano, inaugurano grandi occhiali neri (graduati), al posto delle lenti con montatura invisibile, di effetto deprimente, e comprano in fretta deliziose cravatte: si ritrovano pieni di curiosità dimenticate, lei che conosce tutti, cara signora, perchè non mi fa incontrare Anna Magnani? E l'altra sera abbiamo pranzato con il Senatore Angiolillo, che caro ragazzo, Renato, talmente dinamico.

\*

Ci sono le sciocche: se tu sapessi che nostalgia, le mie care montagne, il mio mare, il lago. Ci sono le sagge: niente zanzare, niente pioggia, niente mosche, e almeno dieci osterie nuove, e tre piscine appena inaugurate. Ci sono le zelanti: la mattina sto due ore davanti alla finestra aperta, per prendere la tintarella. Ci sono le raffinate: dal momento che sto in città, rimarrò bianca, da cittadina.

\*

A Parigi come a Roma, a Nuova York come a Londra l'estate muta le persone, le abitudini, i luoghi, le prospettive delle strade, le particolarità dei caratteri. E la sera, ma pensa, cenavamo in riva all'Aniene, un posto delizioso, con Carla e Adriano, e i due Fossi. Era delizioso, il pollo alla diavola, Adriano si era sciolto, parlava sempre di sè, Carla si era calmata, stava sempre a sentire gli altri. E i due Fossi sembravano guariti dai reumatismi. Era delizioso. Poi, non so, in autunno ci siamo persi di vista, e l'Aniene ha perfino straripato.

\*

Tutti amano, sinceramente, la musica, d'estate. Avremo dei concerti a Versailles. E l'Opera a Caracalla. Mozart a Pitti. Wagner a Piazza San Marco. Torrenti di suoni e di luna avvolgono, carezzevolmente quanti di solito accettano unicamente un film, e possibilmente non musicale. E nelle strade del centro, dure, lisce, canyon di pietre e cemento, scorrono ruscelli di armonie economiche e stupende, la radio del professore, il grammofono del ragioniere.        IRENE BRIN

CLELIA VENTURI                                           GATTINONI

SALOMON          GATTINONI          MONTORSI

*Tailleur in lana nera, gonna ad anfora, giacca con baschina a financhi imbottiti. Colletto e risvolti in volpe argentata.*   *Princesse in crespella di lana nera. Gonna a fuoco addoppiato sul fianco; guarnizione di passamaneria annodata a fiocco.*   *Carpetto in velluto verdone, gonna a ombrello in lana scozzese nera, rossa, verde; sciolletto scozzese, con frangia.*

23

"Giornate romane fra pioggia e sole," text by Irene Brin, illustrations by Brunetta. From *Bellezza*, yr. III, no. 24-25, 1947. Courtesy Accademia di Costume e di Moda, Rome. Donated by Irene Brin

LIBRI                ANTONELLI              BATTILOCCHI

*Redingote doppio petto, in duvetine nera, gonna campana, vita di vespa accentuatissima. Grande colletto in volpe azzurra.*   *Princesse in lana con bordini in velluto. Collarotta, vita di vespa, gonna a innumerevoli spicchi montata con risvolta.*   *Mantello in nero con balza in volpe argentata disposta a spirale. Piccolo colletto in tessuto, grandi paisi in volpe.*

22

DA GRAN SERA: SENZA SPALLINE IN RASO VERDE PALLIDO, DRAPPEGGIATO; GONNA IN RASO COLOR CANELLA,
AMPIEZZA A STRASCICO AMMASSATA DIETRO.

LA BOUTIQUE

*La Boutique. Un abito da pranzo, la gonna in raso biondo dal profilo "a prova",
la giacchettina a righe nere e bionde con baschina posteriore a scatolo, ideata
dalla principessa Lola Giovanelli - Palmer. Accordi in tonalità cangianti: corpetto*

LUCIANA                    BOUTIQUE                    FRATTEGIANI

Di Luciana: spilloni in oro e pietre colorate; oro e perle. Tremor in metallo dorato ornato di stelle. Pettine con tre catenelle pendenti che
reggono grossi diamanti. Della Boutique: collana a battaglione, fili di perle inestate a rete e goccie di pietre verdi. Borsetta da sera in raso
ricamata di strass, rebaldi e perle. Clip a forma di ananas. Di Frattegiani: sandali d'oro, scarpette nere, chiuse, tacco in ceramica.

CLELIA VENTURI              GAUTURON              GAUTURON

Come un ombrello a quattro spicchi il grande berretto in velluto, punto dritto e piatto, di Clelia Venturi. Gli spicchi sono uniti gli uni agli
altri con grosgrain; veletta annodata sotto il mento, tinottuono; cappellino in maglia di lana calzato a mezza testa; veretta con fiocco che scende
da un lato. In alto: piccola toarsa in velluto nero con grossi spilloni a perla e cascata di veletta; arcobaleno di Chantilly.

Irene Brin in her apartment, photo by Pasquale De Antonis,
1951. Courtesy Archivio De Antonis, Rome

# La casa specchio di due personaggi contemporanei

Protetta dalle antiche mura del palazzo paterno di via Bocca di Leone la casa di Irene e Gasparo dal Corso è un'isola di quiete che bilancia il ritmo accelerato della loro vita. Tuttavia nella calma delle spaziose stanze i telefoni squillano continuamente dalla libreria al soggiorno, dalla sala da pranzo alle camere da letto. Le chiamate giungono da ogni parte del mondo, amici e collaboratori in contratti di Irene e Gasparo oltre Oceano si annunciano il loro arrivo, altri invece li attendono all'altro capo del globo al loro prossimo viaggio.

Dalla loro base, Roma, essi partono con disinvoltura senza pari per viaggi che seguono itinerari elaborati e minuziosi in paesi lontani; ovunque fanno scoperte e incontri interessantissimi nel campo dell'arte e del giornalismo. Al ritorno li attende la loro bella casa tranquilla una vita in ogni ambiente per quello di Irene e Gasparo, da abili intenditori, vi hanno raccolto e ancora vi portano: pezzi d'eccezione, opere d'arte. E in questa cornice di cose preziose hanno inserito con spregiudicatezza gli oggetti più curiosi, i piacevoli ricordi dei molti viaggi.

In stanza in stanza Irene con la sua garbatissima sommessa voce racconta, presenta e svela i segreti, le peripezie d'ogni cosa e tutto attorno a noi si anima di particolare interesse.

18

19

20

nelle stanze quadri e oggetti

raccontano i viaggi e

gli itinerari intellettuali dei padroni di casa

21

# Piccole astuzie domestiche

La mia amica Virginia Campbell possiede un magnifico volume rilegato — e lavabile in ogni sua parte — con 366 triplici menus, per la prima colazione, per la seconda e per il pranzo. Questi menus tengono conto delle stagioni, delle festività, delle vacanze, e sono abbastanza elastici da ammettere qualche ulteriore fantasia se ci fossero ospiti. La cuoca, quando viene assunta in servizio, riceve il libro in consegna e non ha altri problemi, Virginia è libera di dipingere, scrivere, dirigere il suo teatro di marionette, con eleganza elegante. Le fragole ed i carciofi, il tacchino e l'agnello si alternano, armoniosamente, sulla sua mensa ed ogni vivanda sarà gustata ad un anno di distanza, più o meno. Infatti i frequenti viaggi dell'intera famiglia consentono qualche spostamento, il menù del 3 aprile viene servito il 28, quando Virginia torna da Chicago, e quello del 6 novembre si presenterà invece un mese dopo. Così anche la sensazione di ineluttabilità, di previgenza, è abolita, e nessuno può stabilire la data esatta attraverso lo sformato di piselini. Meno organizzata di Virginia, io non vado mai oltre una settimana, ed il martedì decido tutto quello che deve avvenire in casa nostra, compreso l'imprevisto. Come quasi tutti i romani noi pranziamo spesso fuori, la sera, con gli amici; se stiamo in casa mangiamo davanti alla TV, su dei vassoi individuali d'argento, sorretti da appositi treppiedi, versione un poco raffinata dei vassoi da ospedale. Infatti il domestico porta i due vassoi completi, dal bicchiere per cocktail fino al lavadita, il minestrone di verdure, le uova alla Bisca, le paste lesse sono sistemati in diverse ciotoline pirofile che serbano il calore e ci permettono di mangiare tranquillamente. Ci capita di finire la frutta dopo il telegiornale, e naturalmente a quell'ora i vassoi li mettiamo via da soli. Un sistema simile ci serve per godersi una terrazza altissimi sui tetti, le sere d'estate, senza costringere il domestico a salire e scendere innumerevoli volte; abbiamo in terrazza un frigidaire ed un armadio per le stoviglie e le apparecchiature, ed utilizziamo ciascuno un piatto di portata per antipasti, allineando nei diversi scomparti l'insalata di riso, il musciame genovese, la caponatina siciliana, le cipolle ripiene e gli sfellanti fichi bianchi, dal loro cuore scarlatto.

I nostri pranzi sono dunque solitari, parchi e pigri. Le nostre colazioni, al contrario, si svolgono con la massima rapidità per consentire a mio marito ed ai due, tre, quattro amici che ci fanno compagnia di tornare ai loro lavori senza sentirsi appesantiti: la nostra tavola rotonda non ammette che sei commensali, se siamo in molti adoperiamo la sala pranzo formale, con due tavoli rettangolari per sei o per otto. Gli amici intimissimi vengono da noi abbastanza spesso perché la mia cuoca cerchi di rinnovare il suo repertorio in maniera da non annoiarli con ripetizioni, anche se, talvolta, ci troviamo di fronte un problema immutabile, la loro dieta dimagrante, il loro regime stabilito dal medico, la dissociazione e l'idiosincrasia. Il dilemma peggiore ci viene posto dalla domenica, perché mio marito ed i suoi amici passano la mattinata a Porta Portese, il romano mercato aux puces, e rincasano ad una qualsiasi ora salata fra le dodici e (Peeviva, non abbiamo trovato nulla», e le quindici («Occasioni stupende, chi aveva voglia di guardare l'orologio!»). Una soluzione domestiche può essere:

*Carciofi al curry:* 2 carciofi romaneschi a persona, ridotti alle foglie tenerissime, bolliti, ricoperti d'una bechamelle densa, al curry, tenuti in forno tiepidissimo dispirotiepido, caldissimo negli ultimi minuti;

*Boeuf Bourguignon:* un bel pezzo di manzo senz'osso tagliato a pezzi larghi e grossi quanto una larga e grossa bistecca fiorentina. Disporre i pezzi (due a testa), in un recipiente di metallo porcellanato, le cui pareti furono già rivestite di lardo a fettine, il cui fondo è coperto di: carote, cipolle, porri e funghetti, a fettine ed a dadi, timo, lauro, prezzemolo, aglio. Questo trito va preparato con molta abbondanza perché lo si colloca, a strati, fra una bistecca e l'altra, ciascuna vigorosamente salata e pepata. Mescolare madera e cognac e con questo liquido riempire la pentola per un terzo. Coprire l'ultimo strato di carne e trito con una larga fetta di lardo. Chiudere ermeticamente il coperchio, con un giro di pasta cruda. Far sobbollire un attimo, e lasciar cuocere dolcemente per cinque ore (se Porta Portese non ha trattenuto il gruppo degli antiquari), ma anche per sette ore (se Porta Portese era affascinante), senza mai alzare il coperchio. L'amico migliore avrà poi il privilegio di scoperchiare e di aspirare il meraviglioso odore.

(Continua a pag. 54) — Irene Brin

(Continua a pag. 54)

dall'alto in basso:

*La terrazza con vista su Trinità dei Monti. Il tavolo di travertino è apparecchiato con un servizio all'americana di Norman Marcus, stampato a motivi di ispirazione peruviana, e con piatti inox tory-wood delle isole Hawaii. Al centro un torito peruviano.*

*Una piccola cucina dove i padroni di casa e i loro amici cucinano pranzi improvvisati. Nello scaffale è pronto per la consultazione una piccola biblioteca internazionale. Anche in questa stanza si trovano dipinti e disegni di Calder, di Mirò, di Clave e di Ignoti del sec. XIX.*

*Nella saletta da pranzo il papier peint Martinique, riveste tutte le pareti. Sulla tavola, dell'800 inglese come le sedie, è disposto, oltre allo scaldavivande inglese giorgiano, vasellame della Compagnia delle Indie. Vasi di Giarra a forma di teste sono allineati lungo le finestre-serra.*

24

25

*Nella camera da letto le porte dipinte a marmo giallo con striature viola chiaro si inseriscono felicemente nel moire giallo chiaro che riveste le pareti. Di moire giallo è anche la coperta del letto, uno splendido esemplare del XVII secolo. Sulla commode Luigi XVI in legno di rosa due reliquiari del '700, due coppe Meig e un cavallo Wei; alla parete un Cristo di Marcello Muccini.*

mobili antichi e oggetti tradizionali
accostati con spregiudicatezza
alle forme più nuove dell'arte

*Vivaci contrasti nella stanza dei disegni. Il letto e la poltrona sono foderati in plaid bianco e nero; la lampada è rossa. Sulla parete verde scuro prendono evidenza disegni di Vespignani, Brunetta, Dereh Hill, Café, Piletti, Muccini.*

*Nella camera da letto un camino impero in mosaico romano ed un armadio con ante dipinte, impero. Nell'interno trova posto una scrivania ribaltabile e tutto quanto riguarda il lavoro giornalistico di Irene Brin. Sul tavolino una scultura di Giuditta Scalini. Sulla parete da sinistra, dipinti e disegni di William Congdon, Picasso, Buffet e Jaulensky. Accanto al letto uno scaffale per dischi e riviste.*

22

23

*previous pages*
"La casa specchio di due personaggi contemporanei," photos by Fortunato
Scrimali and "Piccole astuzie domestiche," text by Irene Brin. From *Novità*,
no. 135, January 1962

Thank-you note with drawing by Fabrizio Clerici dedicated to Irene Brin.
Courtesy Fondi Storici, Galleria Nazionale d'Arte Moderna, Rome
On December 16, 1952, Irene Brin and Gaspero del Corso opened an
exhibition at the Obelisco devoted to "Cats." Many people took part, artists
and others, making contributions in a wide variety of styles but which
all shared a love for the dear domestic cat. Among the many works on show
were lithographs by Bonnard, etchings by Chagall, an *Arliquin au chat*
by Antoni Clavé and drawings by Fabrizio Clerici, Bruno Caruso,
Colombotto Rosso and Leonor Fini. "In the window, but only on the day
of the private view, the most beautiful cats in Rome played happily, under
the eyes of the passersby. I had to call the police. The Roman critics wrote:
'L'Obelisco has ended up as was expected, at the zoo.'"
(From Irene Brin, *1952, L'Italia che esplode*, [unpublished], p. 115)

Qualche pezzo della collezione trousses, il solo "peso inutile" un guardaroba funzionale. Ma trousses di Irene Brin hanno storia. Quella in prezioso legno sandalo e giada fu comprata a Singapore; quella settecentesca, di M sonier è un "servizio da lavoro" sformato in "servizio da bellezza" Giuliana Camerino. Infine, qu indiana è stata lavorata da un a giano di Jaipur. Sotto, a sinistra pesce sacrificale del Nepal, in turchesi e granate è diventato trousse per opera del gioiell Furst di Roma. Anatroccola diana ravvivata con arabeschi oro e d'argento, e la colomba Salvator Dalì in oro e argento, fu una specie di ripicca contro colomba di Picasso. Qui a des la palla in cristalli, di Giuli Fratti, contiene cipria, rossette portaprofumi. La scatola di mac perla e coralli fu comprata nel M sico; il pittore inglese Sutclitte dipinto il ritratto della "gatta dei a manti" sul coperchio di una sc letta "porta-oggetti indispensabil

malarica, gli johd-purs!" Quando si entra nella fantasia e nello sper- pero, non ci sono limiti. Atteni- amoci, invece, a quelli del viaggio vero, del peso lecito. Il mio pro- gramma attuale era: partenza da Roma per Tokio con la Rotta Po-

# HO SCELTO UN GUARDAROB
# PER IL GIRO DEL MOND

Irene Brin's clutch bags. From Irene Brin, "Ho scelto un guardaroba per il giro del mondo," in *Bellezza*, yr. XIX, no. 5, May 1959. Courtesy Accademia di Costume e di Moda, Rome. Donated by Irene Brin. "Salvador Dalí. In April 1952 I met him in Piazza Barberini, his back straight, with his turned-up moustache and his stick: 'Irèèèèèèèène! Tu l'as toujours ton truc?' I took out of my bag the silver dove, trimmed with gold, that I used as powder compact, pillbox and lipstick holder. Designed by Dalí, signed by Dalí, a souvenir of my labors for Dalí: 'Ah, but you must rrrrreturn it to me!" Dalí rolled all his r's in the Spanish manner, whatever language he was speaking. 'Don't use it any more, I have to put in rrrrunning water for you!'" (From Irene Brin, *1952, L'Italia che esplode*, [unpublished], p. 52)

Photographic print, photo by Gaspero del Corso.
From Irene Brin, "Italia a Punta del Este,"
in *Bellezza*, no. 4, April 1952. Courtesy Fondi
Storici, Galleria Nazionale d'Arte Moderna, Rome

Fabiani dresses, silver bromide photographic
print, photo by Pasquale
De Antonis. From "Operazione 'Giro del
Mondo,'" in *Bellezza*, June 1955. Courtesy
Archivio De Antonis, Rome

Simonetta dress, silver bromide photographic
print, photo by Pasquale De Antonis. From
"Operazione 'Giro del Mondo,'" in *Bellezza*, June
1955. Courtesy Archivio De Antonis, Rome

# I COMPONENTI L'"ITALIAN PARADE" A SYDNEY

Sono presenti alla Parata della Moda Italiana in Australia, anche molte "Boutiques" note e fra queste la Merving, di Torino.

Fra i modelli che la David Jones ha scelto da Schubert a Roma, figurerà questa redingote di cotone turchese con risvolti bianchi.

Da Carosa è stato scelto, fra altri, un mantello che riportò successo alla presentazione di Firenze, variato nel colore: rosa chiaro.

Un "due pezzi" da sera in jersey di Mirsa: bianco, tempestato di pailletles, fitte e rade.

Nel numero dei pezzi in jersey di Mirsa che gli esperti australiani hanno trovato interessanti, figura questo insieme con cappuccio.

Di Elsa Volpe figurano nell'Italian parade, tre modelli, da giorno e da sera. Fra gli abiti da giorno, questo, in shantung di seta rosso.

La preferenza è andata, come si può notare a diversi tipi di abito-mantello. Fra i modelli di Carosa è stato scelto anche questo.

Molti gli stampati in seta pura. Di Carosa questo "due pezzi" in pura seta di Toninelli.

Irene Brin, "Partiti per l'Australia. L'Italian Parade a Sidney," in *Bellezza*, yr. XV, no. 6, June 1955. Courtesy Accademia di Costume e di Moda, Rome. Donated by Irene Brin

Quick-change outfit by Antonelli, photo by Fortunato Scrimali. From Irene Brin, "Estate italiana in Australia," in *Bellezza*, yr. XV, no. 6, June 1955. Courtesy Accademia di Costume e di Moda, Rome. Donated by Irene Brin

Emilio Pucci dresses, photo by Fortunato Scrimali. From Irene Brin, "Partiti per l'Australia," in *Bellezza*, yr. XV, no. 6, June 1955. Courtesy Accademia di Costume e di Moda, Rome. Donated by Irene Brin

EMILIO PUCCI

opelli di paglia simili a giganteschi fiori subacquei, il paesaggio roccioso velato dall'acqua che s'infrange contro gli scogli e le tinte dei costumi vaga-
contribuiscono a dare a questa scena l'impressione di un fondale sottomarino. In realtà si tratta di due modelli da spiaggia di Emilio Pucci foto-
i in Sicilia nel gennaio di quest'anno. Rosa pallido con maglietta nera ornata di rosso corallo l'uno; color aragosta con scollatura bordata in viola l'altro.
mbi i costumi sono in gabardine cotton textiloses e fanno parte dell'acquisto di numerosi modelli "Emilio" fatti per la vendita in Australia.

# ARTITI PER L'AUSTRALIA

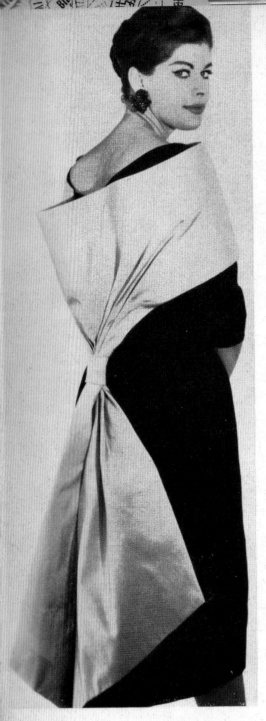

La sci
pottin
re da "
tussor

De Luca shawl. From Irene Brin,
"Ho scelto un guardaroba per il giro
del mondo," in *Bellezza*, yr. XIX, no.
5, May 1959. Courtesy Accademia
di Costume e di Moda, Rome.
Donated by Irene Brin

"Linea Utamaro" dresses by De Luca
chosen by Irene Brin for her trip
to Japan. From Irene Brin,
"Ho scelto un guardaroba per il giro
del mondo," in *Bellezza*, yr. XIX,
no. 5, May 1959. Courtesy Accademia
di Costume e di Moda, Rome.
Donated by Irene Brin

*collaboratrice, Irene Brin, ha fatto per la seconda volta il giro del*
*Le abbiamo chiesto tutti i dettagli precisi dell'eccezionale bagaglio che*
*portato con sé per essere quella giornalista aggiornatissima dei minimi*
*particolari di moda e quella "penna" d'ineguagliabile spirito che è*

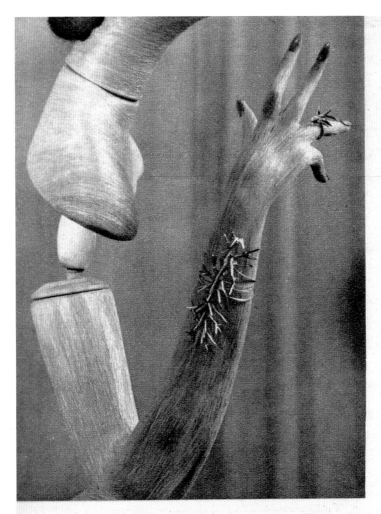

*« 3 P » è lo Studio per creazione di gioielli*
*moderni che ha ideato questo bracciale in oro*
*con anello analogo per la presentazione di*
*uno dei manichini Rosa, inviati a Sydney.*

Pink dummies. From "In viaggio anche i manichini made in Italy,"
in *Bellezza*, yr. xv, no. 6, June 1955. Courtesy Accademia di Costume
e di Moda, Rome. Donated by Irene Brin

Bruno Caruso, *Portrait of Irene Brin*, 1960,
pencil on paper

Donna Marella Caracciolo Agnelli. From
"Beauty in Our Times", photo
by Richard Avedon, in *Harper's Bazaar*,
April 1954. Courtesy Accademia
di Costume e di Moda, Rome. Donated
by Irene Brin

Mrs. Leopold Stokowski. From "Beauty in
Our Times", photo by Richard Avedon,
in *Harper's Bazaar*, April 1954. Courtesy
Accademia di Costume e di Moda, Rome.
Donated by Irene Brin

RICHARD AVEDON

## Beauty in Our Times

• To certain people at certain times in history, the pink rose has seemed the
single standard of beauty: a tranquil and naive ideal—and a strangely
limiting one it would seem to us today. For we are fortunate
to live in an era of great movement and event, of almost unrivaled discovery.
And so it is that our eyes are opened to many perceptions of beauty.
In our theatre, our films and novels and in our lives, it is no longer the
vision of a young woman of twenty that dominates us. Beauty in a woman
presents itself to us at all ages; and as something more than a
bright eye and a pure profile. Not only are we pleasurably affected

Kitty Hawks. From "Beauty in Our
Times", photo by Richard Avedon, in
*Harper's Bazaar*, April 1954. Courtesy
Accademia di Costume e di Moda, Rome.
Donated by Irene Brin

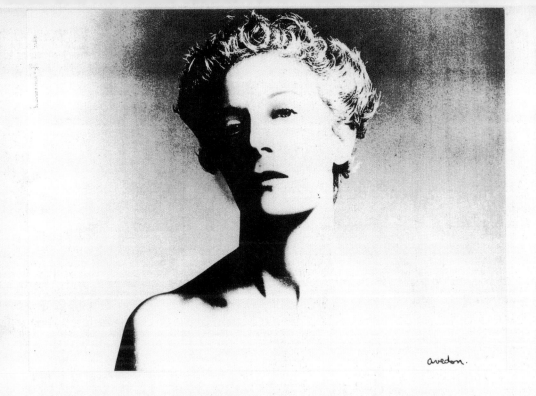

avedon.

RICHARD AVEDON

Contessa Madina Arrivabene (above) moves
in an aura of the complete romantic, has the romantic looks o
fair Venetian. Her blond and silver hair floats carelessly about

Portrait of Irene Brin, photo
by Richard Avedon, 1950s

Countess Madina Arrivabene. From
"Beauty in Our Times," photo by Richard
Avedon, in *Harper's Bazaar*, April 1954.
Courtesy Accademia di Costume
e di Moda, Rome. Donated by Irene Brin

*Happy Christmas*
*from*
*The Snows*

*The Snow Happy Christmas*, Carmel Snow with
her family. Courtesy Fondi Storici, Galleria
Nazionale d'Arte Moderna, Rome

*Happy Christmas from*
*The Snows*

10

y are
sheep
sm to
for a
nno's
hat a
they
ening
o that
and
a you
is no
very-
ldren
at in
ome-
ideed

s and
ight,

bove
umor
from

n the
kings
80)

"Christmas in Scanno," photos by Henry Cartier-Bresson. From
*Harper's Bazaar*, December 1955. Courtesy Accademia
di Costume e di Moda, Rome. Donated by Irene Brin

i, yesterday
le of Scanno
r own. They
ples, nor the
heat in the
er of the in-
r in Rome—
m.
Scanno, you
ook down at
s man has a
o down into
do before he
nd of stone,
t steep slope
it from slip-
canno if you
e post office,
there is no
d to live al-
ill find men
ntine, in the
also to leave

l women of
of the town
are dressed
capes round
ntain night.
silver when
e decorated
. Three old
o the altar;
y sit on the
waiting for
ir black felt
yone is talk-
l vestments;
s. The three
om for him;
s, makes the
d the Child
o the altar.

Simonetta and Fabiani dresses, photo by Louise Dahl-Wolfe. From "The
Long Daylight Evenings," in *Harper's Bazaar*, June 1955. Courtesy
Accademia di Costume e di Moda, Rome. Donated by Irene Brin

# The Long Daylight Evenings

• This year's delicious sequel to long sun-filled days

Drawing of Irene Brin. From Irene Brin, "Cronache dei ridotti," in *Maschere*, yr. I, no. 2, February 15, 1945. Courtesy Fondi Storici, Galleria Nazionale d'Arte Moderna, Rome

Drawing of Irene Brin. From Irene Brin, "Music Hall," in *Maschere*, yr. I, no. 3, February 28, 1945. Courtesy Fondi Storici, Galleria Nazionale d'Arte Moderna, Rome

"Carnet mondano," illustrations by Brunetta, in *Bellezza*, yr. XIV, no. 4, April 1954. Courtesy Accademia di Costume e di Moda, Rome. Donated by Irene Brin

# A PARIGI durante le collezioni

CKTAIL DA CHARLES SIMONI E BERT BARGER DELLA CASA FATH

Rrinsky
Roger Vivier
Dessès
Mme Selmer
Elsa Schiaparelli
Rina Redrini
Gaspero Dal Corso
Irene Brin
Brofferio
Jacquy
Pierre Monchicourt
Mme Janine Cusin
Robert Cusin
Simone
Charles Simoni
Jacques Fath
Madame Jean Bénédick
Patricia
Mme Christiane
M.lle Olga
M.lle Charlotte

Mme Althaus de la Radio Diffusion Suisse et journaux de Berne
da "Schiaparelli"

chez FRINGHIAM
collier baguettes diamants brillants et 24 rubis.

Elsa Robiola
Fiore
Giorgio Sansa
Sandro Volta
Campolonghi
Signora Volta
Bonaventura Caloro corrispondente di TEMPO
Florentine
Il corrispondente di Gazzetta Sera -Torino

PRANZO DI GIORNALISTI AL FLORENCE

Mme Antoine
M.lle Renée Lecadre
da Grés
Mme Vionnet
da Griffe

Simone Baron
Comtsse Toulouse Lautrec
Lucien François
Mme Lebidois
Michel DeBrunhoff
Donati
Viviane de Gray mour
Mme Bricard
Carmen Snow
Dior
Mme Luling
Mme Genevois
da Dior

brunetta

49

osa.
imi
In
*ato
*cato
*ua,
*cato
*sul-
*cco-
*ige.

Model by Sarmi for Elizabeth Arden. From Irene Brin, "Immobilità e fantasia di New York," in *Bellezza*, yr. XV, no. 1, January 1955. Courtesy Accademia di Costume e di Moda, Rome. Donated by Irene Brin. "Ever since Ferdinando Sarmi left Italy and gave up his activity as a designer for the cinema (we have him to thank for the best clothes ever to have appeared on our screens, the ones worn by Lucia Bosé in *Cronaca di un amore*), he has lived in New York, where he is in charge of Elizabeth Arden's high fashion department. Thus he has had an opportunity to get to know the needs, the whims, the instincts and even the physical measurements and moral qualities, of American patrician women. No one knows better than he what a suit should be like, how a dinner dress can be: the first collection that bears Sarmi's name has been a complete success. We would like to derive from this highly successful career a formula that would be of use to Italian creators who have stayed in Italy, and who are so often troubled by the need to guess in advance what American buyers are looking for. For Nando Sarmi it's plain sailing, since he is in daily contact with the real women for whom his clothes are intended and not, as happens over here, with their phantoms." (From Irene Brin, "A New York: un italiano che ha capito l'America," in *Bellezza*, no. 8, 1959)

Fontana dress, photo by Derujinsky. From "Have you seen… Have you heard…," in *Harper's Bazaar*, June 1958. Courtesy Accademia di Costume e di Moda, Rome. Donated by Irene Brin

BIKI

BERTOLI

BELLAVITE

FRATTI

CONT, VENEZIANE

"TOPAZE"

EMILIA BELLINI

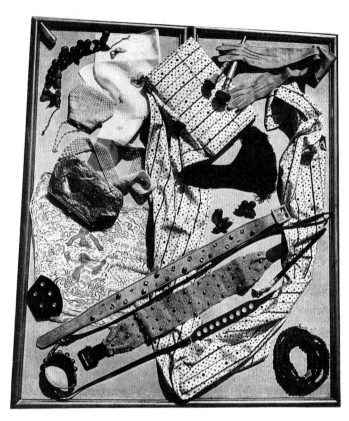

## Distillato di accessori fantasia

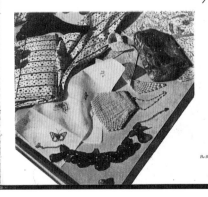

Bellezza-Parts

Biki: la borsettina da sera e il collier a nastro di perle; i guanti di camoscio nero con polso orlato di frangia; il portacipria in camoscio nero con enormi diamanti incastonati • Franco Bertoli: la borsetta-sciarpa, in taffetas bianco a coriandoli e righe nere. È una sciarpa molto lunga che finisce con una busta. Modello brevettato e depositato. Impugnature autentiche del Settecento, in tormalina rosa, oro e madreperla, oro e porcellana con miniatura; avorio cesellato, per ombrellini moderni • Bellavite: i guanti da sera, lunghissimi, in capretto "glacé" color limone • Fratti: le cinture in spago, in juta, in pelle dorata, con pietre colorate o perle; la parure "Pomona", creazione 1949, in frutta di pristal • Conterie Veneziane: la borsetta in raso, perle, stras e coralli; la collana a più giri di perle ghiacciate, verdi e rosse. • "Topaze" Venezia: fazzoletto in chiffon dipinto a mano su disegno di F. Pallavicini • Emilia Bellini: fazzoletto in mussola di lino bianco, farfalle ricamate al naturale.

47

"Distillate of patterned accessories," from *Bellezza*, no. 4, April 1949. Courtesy Accademia di Costume e di Moda, Rome. Donated by Irene Brin

"Selection of accessories." From *Bellezza*, yr. II, no. 12-13, December 1946. Courtesy Accademia di Costume e di Moda, Rome. Donated by Irene Brin

*Mr. John's*

### 1953 FALL & WINTER COLLECTION
### ROMANCE in VENICE

Mr. John brochure, *Romance in Venice*, fall/winter 1953. Courtesy Fondi Storici, Galleria Nazionale d'Arte Moderna, Rome

In her role as interpreter and popularizer of the international culture of fashion, Irene Brin did her best to draw the Italian public's attention to the creations of the American milliner Mr. John, who, in the early fifties, chose Venice and its cultural heritage, visual as well as literary, as the setting in which to construct and present his collections.
Like authentic fetishes, those hats came to represent the magic worked on the female American tourist of the fifties by the city of Venice.
Irene Brin had already reflected on the tendency to assign the status of a souvenir to the garment or accessory at the end of the forties:
"'Let's go to the Venice Festival' we announced in 1935, and put on golden sandals. Filippo Secchi may remember sitting with me and Raffaele Calzini on the chairs at the Florian, which he had taken from the tables where they had been stacked up, one night in 1935: we had come from Lido by motorboat, after seeing a movie of which I recall nothing, in the Giardino delle Fontane. The square was deserted, white in the moonlight [...]. I was wearing a dress in a style that was common then, a white Indian sari, bordered with gold, completed by drapery wrapped around the body, and to me it didn't seem common at all, but in a way magical, intended to reveal a different me, perhaps a happy one. [...] Who knows what Giorgio Prosperi and Gino Visentini will remember of 1946? Then one day a particular image comes to mind, not necessarily a cinematographic one but almost always comprising a witty and attractive critic in the act of doing up a sandal against the wall decorated with the poster for *Anche il boia muore ammazzato*. Then the festival will have become history."
(From Irene Brin, "End del Festival," in *Film Rivista*, year III, September 30, 1946)

Mr. John collection, *Romance in Venice*, fall/winter 1953. Courtesy Fondi Storici, Galleria Nazionale d'Arte Moderna, Rome

Fabiani dress. From Romeo Toninelli (ed.), *Venezia moda e costume*, photo by Wender and Pozzi Bellini, Centro Internazionale delle Arti e del Costume, 1956. Courtesy Fondi Storici, Galleria Nazionale d'Arte Moderna, Rome

Simonetta dress. From Romeo Toninelli (ed.), *Venezia moda e costume*, photo by Wender and Pozzi Bellini, Centro Internazionale delle Arti e del Costume, 1956. Courtesy Fondi Storici, Galleria Nazionale d'Arte Moderna, Rome

Marucelli dress. From Romeo Toninelli (ed.), *Venezia moda e costume*, photo by Wender and Pozzi Bellini, Centro Internazionale delle Arti e del Costume, 1956. Courtesy Fondi Storici, Galleria Nazionale d'Arte Moderna, Rome

Antonelli dress. From Romeo Toninelli (ed.), *Venezia moda e costume*, photo by Wender and Pozzi Bellini, Centro Internazionale delle Arti e del Costume, 1956. Courtesy Fondi Storici, Galleria Nazionale d'Arte Moderna, Rome

MINGOLINI - GUGENHEIM
ROMA

TSUNE SAKAI - KYOTO

Mingolini-Guggenheim dress. From
Romeo Toninelli (ed.), *Venezia moda
e costume*, photo by Wender and Pozzi
Bellini, Centro Internazionale delle Arti e
del Costume, 1956. Courtesy Fondi Storici,
Galleria Nazionale d'Arte Moderna, Rome

Tsune Sakai-Kyoto dress. From Romeo
Toninelli (ed.), *Venezia moda e costume*,
photo by Wender and Pozzi Bellini, Centro
Internazionale delle Arti e del Costume,
1956. Courtesy Fondi Storici, Galleria
Nazionale d'Arte Moderna, Rome

Massimo Campigli, *Portrait of Irene Brin*, 1954, oil on canvas.
From Bruno Mantura, Patrizia Rosazza Ferraris (eds.), *Massimo Campigli*. Milan: Electa, 1994.
"Campigli, who had often shown at L'Obelisco, painted this portrait in 1954. Years later, recalling the many times she posed in his study (the never satisfied artist was always beginning her portrait all over again on ever larger canvases), Irene Brin quoted the master's words: '[…] Irene is so Campigliesque that everything becomes too easy, I have to explain her sadness.'"
(From Patrizia Rosazza Ferraris, in B. Mantura, P. Rosazza Ferraris [eds.], *Massimo Campigli*. Milan: Electa, 1994, p. 191)

# BIOGRAPHICAL NOTE

The writer and journalist Irene Brin, pseudonym of Maria Vittoria
Rossi, was born in Rome on June 14, 1911. Her father, a general in
the army assigned to the capital at that time, was Ligurian, from
Sasso di Bordighera, while her mother was of Austrian nationality. A
cultured and austere woman, she passed on to her daughter her
passion for art, literature, travel and the study of foreign languages.
Before settling permanently with her family in Genoa, she spent part
of her childhood in Florence, the city where her beloved sister Franca
was born. In 1932 she had already begun to write society pieces for
the Genoese daily *Il Lavoro*, edited at the time by Giovanni Ansaldo.
The insight into the way the world worked revealed in those first
original and "wry" articles caught the attention of Leo Longanesi. In
1937 the journalist invited her to write for *Omnibus*, a weekly of
political and cultural current affairs that he edited himself from 1937
to 1939. It was Longanesi who suggested she adopt the pseudonym of
Irene Brin: an invented name that would impose itself with the force
of a real one on the long series of *noms de plume* used by the journalist
in the course of her professional career. A selection of the pieces that
appeared in the "Giallo e Rosso" column of *Omnibus* has been
published in the volume *Cose viste 1938-1939*, brought out by
Sellerio in 1994.
Her first article for *Omnibus* appeared on April 12, 1937, on the same
day that Irene Brin married Gaspero del Corso, an officer in the army.
She had met him in Rome, at the Cavalry Ball held at the Grand
Hotel during the Carnival of 1935. Initially they lived together at
Merano, and then moved to Rome, the city that was to see them
become leading figures on the postwar cultural and social scene.
In the May of 1941 the writer joined her husband in Yugoslavia, a
war zone to which Colonel del Corso had been assigned. She stayed
there until the spring of 1943, and recorded her experience of that
difficult time in articles for the magazines *Documento*, *Storia* and *Il
Mediterraneo*. Her journalistic writing, however, was not able to do
full justice to the sensitivity with which Irene Brin had responded to
people, places and situations constantly threatened by the crude logic

of war. That reality inspired thirteen short stories which were collected in the volume *Olga a Belgrado*, published by Vallecchi in December 1943. Back in Italy, Irene Brin and her husband spent the months of the occupation in Rome: she, distant from the editorial offices of the newspapers that had come under German control, wrote only for *La Stampa* and Corrado Alvaro's *Il Popolo di Roma*; he, a dissident and involved in actions against the Germans, gave assistance to political exiles and was soon forced to go underground. At that time her main source of income was from her translation work. The publisher De Fonseca gave her one novel a week to translate, paying her three thousand lire each: it was a lot, but not enough to support the thirty-seven soldiers to whom she and her husband had given refuge in the garrets of their house on Via Bocca di Leone. Together, they took the decision to sell their wedding gifts: "three drawings by Picasso, one by Matisse, a few drawings by de Pisis and a Morandi, very small but radiant and full of gold."[1] These works and some valuable volumes from their personal library were put on sale at the small art gallery and antiquarian bookstore on Via Bissolati, La Margherita, which Irene Brin agreed to run for a percentage of the proceeds. The gallery was a meeting place for many artists and intellectuals of the time, from Luchino Visconti to Massimo Girotti, Renato Guttuso, Renzo Vespignani and the entire Portonaccio group. The rich human and cultural experience gained at the art gallery did not remain an isolated fact in Irene Brin's life. Leaving La Margherita after it was put up for sale, the del Corsos, thanks to a modest inheritance from the journalist's father, inaugurated the Galleria dell'Obelisco, at Via Sistina 146, with an exhibition devoted to Morandi in the fall of 1946. The opening of the gallery gave them the opportunity to play the concrete role of cultural mediators: they "exported" the new artists of postwar Italy and "imported" great foreign artists, excluded from Italy during the "provincial" years of Fascism. Thus they helped to launch young Italian artists like Music, Burri, Afro, Mirko and Vespignani on the art market. In 1948 they organized the first overseas exhibition of the American Federation of Art, and at the same time began to bring the works of such important exponents of contemporary art as Dalí, Magritte, Tanguy, Matta, Rauschenberg, Calder and Bacon to Rome. Among the most interesting exhibitions to be held at the Obelisco were: *Neri e Muffe* by Alberto Burri (1952), *Drawings of Mayan Art*, *Magritte*, presented by Libero de Libero, *Scatole e Feticci Personali* by Bob Rauschenberg (1953), *Twenty Imaginary Views of the American Scene by Twenty Young Italian Artists* (1953), *The Picasso of Moscow* (1954), *Alexander Calder*, presented by Giulio Carlo Argan (1955).

For Irene Brin the experience of the Obelisco was not just the fulfillment of a long cherished passion for the visual arts, but functioned as a real catalyst for her cultural interests and activities. The numerous journeys she undertook to stage exhibitions in Rome and abroad were not only an expression of her active engagement on the front of the visual arts, but served to promote Italian culture: from literature to the cinema and fashion.

The voice of this writer and cultural intermediary would be modulated at different times, and under different circumstances, with wisdom, stinging irony and chameleon-like sensibility, as if in response to the need to present herself in guises and roles that were constantly changing, but always effective in performing a constructive function with respect to the social and cultural transformations that were to bring the country into the modern world over the course of the fifties and sixties.

Irene Brin became a familiar figure to the public at large in the guise, from 1950 to 1969, of the Central European noblewoman Countess Clara Ràdjanny von Skévitch, who put all her consummate art of living at the service of the readers of the *Settimana Incom* in the famous advice column entitled "Consigli". Following in the footsteps of the "Letters from the Shy" published in *Il Secolo Illustrato* in the forties, "Contessa Clara" dispensed lessons of etiquette from the columns of the weekly. As Contessa Clara, Irene Brin published the volumes *Galateo* (Rome, Colombo, 1953) and *I segreti del successo* (Rome, Colombo, 1954), both anthologized in the posthumous *Dizionario del successo e del insuccesso e dei luoghi comuni* ("Dictionary of Success and Failure and of Commonplaces"; Palermo: Sellerio, 1986). The articles on society and custom in which she had portrayed the lifestyles of the Italians in the years between the two wars were collected in the volume *Usi e costumi 1920-1940*, published in Rome by Luigi Donatello in 1944. This publication, which won her a great deal of praise, was immediately followed by that of *Le Visite* ("The Visits," Partenia, 1945), a collection of a series of short and evocative tales that had already appeared in magazines and newspapers. Irene Brin wrote for innumerable dailies and periodicals, including: *Il Messaggero*, *Il Giornale d'Italia*, *Il Corriere d'Informazione*, *Il Corriere della Sera*, *Film Magazine*, *Maschere*, *Cineillustrato*, *Domus*, *Video - La rivista della televisione* and *Finsider*.

On Italian and international fashion, of which she boasted an extensive knowledge, she wrote for many newspapers and magazines in Italy and abroad, including the international magazine of high fashion *Bellezza*, which published her articles from 1941 to 1968; *Harper's Bazaar*, the American magazine of which she was Rome editor from 1952 to 1969; and the Italian magazines *Grazia*, *Annabella*, *L'Europeo* and *Domina*. On June 2, 1955 she was awarded the honor of Cavaliere Ufficiale dell'Ordine al Merito della Repubblica Italiana ("Knight Officer of the Order of Merit of the Italian Republic") in recognition of her efforts as a journalist in Italy and abroad on behalf of the development and success of Italian fashion in the world.

Irene Brin worked on numerous translations. Among them it is worth singling out: *Prime vite immaginarie*, the Italian edition of Marcel Schwob's *Les vies imaginaires* published by Capriotti Editore (1946); *Vita segreta di Salvador Dalí*, the autobiography of the surrealist artist whose work had been introduced into Italy by the Obelisco, translated for Longanesi in 1949; *Riflessi in un occhio d'oro*, the translation of Carson McCullers's *Reflections in a Golden Eye* for Longanesi in 1963.

In 1968 she wrote an autobiographical account for the Genoese publishing house Immordino: *1952, L'Italia che esplode*. It should have been brought out in the series "365... a year in the life of..." directed by the writer Milena Milani, but was never published.

Irene Brin died of a tumor on May 31, 1969, at Sasso di Bordighera. She had wanted to stay in the much-loved family house on her return from a difficult journey to Strasbourg, undertaken with enthusiasm despite the deterioration in her health, to attend the opening of the exhibition *Les Ballets Russes de Sergej P. Diaghilev*. The Galleria dell'Obelisco had contributed to the staging of the exhibition by

sending an electronic reconstruction of Giacomo Balla's scenery for
the *Firebird*.

Following her death the refined couturier Alberto Fabiani dedicated
his 1970 spring/summer collection to her, addressing words of
affection and esteem to a loyal friend, an elegant woman and an
influential journalist who had always been able to understand, follow
and encourage Italian fashion.

Between the end of the eighties and the beginning of the nineties the
Sellerio publishing house brought out new editions of *Usi e costumi
1920-1940*, *Il dizionario del successo e del insuccesso*, *Le Visite* and *Cose
viste*.

NOTE_____

[1] "Irene Brin e Gaspero del Corso, una intervista all'Obelisco," in *Domus*, 403, June 1963.

Irene Brin, December 1961

# BIBLIOGRAPHY

PRIMARY TEXTS

Articles by Irene Brin published in *Bellezza* and cited in the text:

"Il Nord e il Sud," in *Bellezza*, no. 1 (1945).

"Massima e Minima," in *Bellezza*, no. 4 (1946).

"Passeggiata romana," in *Bellezza*, no. 7 (1946).

"Un altro Obelisco," in *Bellezza*, nos. 12-13 (1946).

"Giornate romane fra pioggia e sole," in *Bellezza*, nos. 24-5 (1947).

"Alla Toulouse Lautrec," in *Bellezza*, nos. 18-19 (1947).

"Salvador Dalí in sartoria," in *Bellezza*, no. 1 (1949).

"Obiettivi puntati sull'Italia," in *Bellezza*, no. 5 (1950).

"Belle donne in serie, abiti belli in serie, ecco la formula della moda americana," in *Bellezza*, no. 9 (1950).

"Sole d'Italia in pieno inverno di Nuova York," in *Bellezza*, no. 2 (1952).

"Italia a Punta del Este," in *Bellezza*, no. 4 (1952).

"Con le attrici italiane a Nuova York," in *Bellezza*, no. 12 (1952).

"Partiti per l'Australia," in *Bellezza*, no. 6 (1955).

"Moda italiana giramondo," in *Bellezza*, no. 4 (1956).

"Incontro internazionale della moda a Venezia," in *Bellezza*, no. 10 (1956).

"Viaggi ben organizzati e guardaroba internazionali," in *Bellezza*, no. 6 (1957).

"Ho scelto un guardaroba per il giro del mondo," in *Bellezza*, no. 5 (1959).

"Best Sellers" in *Bellezza*, no. 10 (1959).

"Biancheria di ieri e di oggi," in *Bellezza*, no. 4 (1960).

"Affrontiamo il Minotauro della moda," in *Bellezza*, no. 6 (1964).


Articles by Irene Brin cited in the text and published in other newspapers, magazines and books:

"Fedeltà di Morella," in *Il Lavoro*, April 23, 1933.

"Occhi socchiusi," in *Il Lavoro*, October 25, 1933.

"Pianto per Jean," in *Il Lavoro*, June 20, 1937.

"Complicità con Dalí," in *Come vi piace* (*As You Like It*), in the version staged by the Compagnia Italiana di Prosa, directed by Luchino Visconti. Roma: Carlo Bestetti Edizioni d'Arte, 1948.

"Fanno loro la vera moda," 1949, from an unidentified periodical, Archivio Irene Brin, La Centrale dell'Arte.

"Sapere raccontare," in *Il Giornale d'Italia*, October 11, 1953.

"Un nome inventato," in *Il Borghese*, yr. VIII, no. 41 (1957).

"Rivelare un genio sì, un amore segreto no," in *Harper's Bazaar Italia* no. 1, 1969.

Published works of Irene Brin:

Irene Brin, *Olga a Belgrado*. Florence: Vallecchi, 1943.

Irene Brin, *Usi e costumi 1920-1940*. Rome: Donatello de Luigi, 1944.

Irene Brin, *Le Visite*. Rome: Casa Editrice Partenia, 1945.

Irene Brin, *Images de Lautrec*. Rome: Carlo Bestetti Edizioni d'arte/Collezione dell'Obelisco, 1947.

Irene Brin, *Femmes de Lautrec*. Rome: Carlo Bestetti. Rome: Edizioni d'arte/Collezione dell'Obelisco, 1954.

Irene Brin, *Il Galateo*. Rome: Colombo Editore, 1953

Irene Brin, *I segreti del successo*. Rome: Colombo Editore, 1954.

Posthumously published works and reprints:

Irene Brin, *Usi e costumi 1920-1940*. Palermo: Sellerio, 1981.

Irene Brin, *Il dizionario del successo e dell'insuccesso*. Palermo: Sellerio, 1986.

Irene Brin, *Le Visite*. Palermo: Sellerio, 1991.

Irene Brin, *Cose viste*. Palermo: Sellerio, 1994.

Unpublished works:

Irene Brin, *1952, L'Italia che esplode*.

## CRITICAL BIBLIOGRAPHY AND ESSAYS ON IRENE BRIN:

MAURIZIA BOSCAGLI, "The Power of Style: Fashion and Self-Fashioning in Irene Brin's Journalistic Writing," in Robin Pickering-Iazzi (ed. by), *Mothers of Invention, Women, Italian Fascism, and Culture*. Minneapolis-London: University of Minnesota Press, 1995.

FEDERICA MERLANTI, "L''armonia bianca e perduta'. Testimonianza e esorcismo della scrittura nell'opera di Irene Brin," in Francesco De Nicola, Pier Antonio Zannoni (eds.), *La fama e il silenzio, Scrittrici dimenticate del primo Novecento*. Venice: Marsilio Editori, 2002.

INDRO MONTANELLI, "Irene Brin," in Id., *Rapaci in cortile*. Milan: Longanesi, 1952.

LIETTA TORNABUONI, "Nota," in Irene Brin, *Usi e Costumi 1920-1940*. Palermo: Sellerio, 1981.

SANDRO VIOLA, "Nota," in Irene Brin, *Il dizionario del successo e dell'insuccesso*. Palermo: Sellerio, 1986.

REVIEWS AND INTERVIEWS ON IRENE BRIN:

ALBERTO ARBASINO, "Contessa che bella rubrica," in *La Repubblica*, June 17, 1981.

"Irene Brin e Gaspero del Corso, un'intervista all'Obelisco," in *Domus*, June 1963.

GIGLIOLA JANNINI, "Nelle vene inchiostro blu," in *Panorama*, June 22, 1981.

LIETTA TORNABUONI, "La giornalista di velluto," in *Alias*, weekly supplement of *Il Manifesto*, August 5, 2000.


FASHION STUDIES:

ALBERTO ABRUZZESE, NELLO BARILE (eds.), *Communifashion. Sulla moda, della comunicazione*. Rome: Luca Sossella Editore, 2001.

EVA PAOLA AMENDOLA (ed. by), *Vestire Italiano, Quarant'anni di moda nelle immagini dei grandi fotografi*. Rome: Edizioni Oberon, 1983.

ASPESI NATALIA, *Il Lusso e l'Autarchia. Storia dell'eleganza italiana, 1930-1944*. Milan: Rizzoli, 1982.

BETTINA BALLARD, *In My Fashion*. New York: David McKay Company, 1960.

ROLAND BARTHES, *Sistema della moda*. Turin: Einaudi, 1970.

–, *Le bleu est à la mode cette année*. Paris: Éditions de L'Institut Français de la Mode, 2001.

–, *Il senso della moda*, ed. by Gianfranco Marrone. Turin: Einaudi, 2006.

–, *The Language of Fashion*, ed by Andy Stafford, Michael Carter. New York-Oxford: Berg, 2006.

CARLO MARCO BELFANTI, FABIO GIUSBERTI (eds.), *Storia d'Italia, annali 19. La moda*. Turin: Einaudi, 2003.

NINA BORGHESE, "Italy," in *Time*, January 29, 1965.

CHRISTOPHER BREWARD, *Fashion*, Oxford-New York: Oxford University Press, 2003.

STELLA BRUZZI, PAMELA CHURCH GIBSON (eds.), *Fashion Cultures*, London-New York: Routledge, 2000.

GRAZIETTA BUTAZZI, *Per una storia della moda pronta*. Florence: Edifir, 1991.

GRAZIETTA BUTAZZI, ALESSANDRA MOTTOLA MOLFINO et al. (eds.), *La moda italiana*. Milan: Electa, 1987.

PATRIZIA CALEFATO, *Mass moda. Linguaggio e immaginario del corpo rivestito*. Genoa: Costa&Nolan, 1996.

ANNA CAMBEDDA, NICOLETTA CARDANO, "Appunti per un discorso sulla moda femminile in Italia tra il 1870 and il 1911," in *I piaceri e i giorni: la moda*, catalogue of the exhibition, *Roma Capitale. 1870-1911*. Venice: Marsilio, 1983.

ANGELA CARTER, "Notes for a Theory of the Sixties Style," in *Nothing Sacred*. London: Virago, 1982.

EDMONDE CHARLES-ROUX, *Chanel*. London: The Harvill Press, 1995.

PAOLA COLAIACOMO, VITTORIA C. CARATOZZOLO (eds.), *Mercanti di stile. Le culture della moda dagli anni '20 a oggi*. Rome: Editori Riuniti, 2002.

FRED DAVIS, *Fashion, Culture, and Identity*. Chicago: University of Chicago Press, 1992.

CHRISTIAN DIOR, *Conférences écrites par Christian Dior pour la Sorbonne, 1955-1957*. Paris: Éditions de l'Institut Français de la Mode/Éditions du Regard, 2003.

JOHN ESTEN, *Diana Vreeland Bazaar Years*. New York: Universe Publishing, 2001.

MARIA LUISA FRISA (ed.), *Lo sguardo italiano. La fotografia italiana di moda dal 1951*. Milan: Edizioni Charta/Fondazione Pitti Immagine Discovery, 2005.

MINNIE GASTEL, *50 anni di moda italiana*. Milan: Avallardi, 1995.

CRISTINA GIORCELLI (ed.), *Abito e identità, Ricerche di storia letteraria e culturale*. Rome: Edizioni Associate, 2 vols., 1995, 1997.

BONIZZA GIORDANI ARAGNO, *Moda romana del 1945 al 1965: Storie di moda*. Rome: De Luca, 1998.

BONIZZA GIORDANI ARAGNO, *900 il secolo alla moda 1900-2001, Sorelle Fontana*, Fondazione Micol Fontana. Rome: Promograph Communication, 2001.

SOFIA GNOLI, *La donna l'eleganza il fascismo*. Catania: Edizioni Del Prisma, 2000.

ANNE HOLLANDER, *Seeing through Clothes*. Berkeley-Los Angeles-London: University of California Press, 1993.

–, "Accounting for Fashion," in Id., *Feeding the Eye*. Berkeley-Los Angeles-London: University of California Press, 1999.

EMILIA KUSTER ROSSELLI, "Alle sorgenti dell'artigianato fiorentino," in *Bellezza*, nos. 18-19, 1947.

VALENTINA LAWFORD, "Pucci The Magnificent," in *Vogue*, March 15, 1965.

KATELL LE BOURHIS, STEFANIA RICCI, LUIGI SETTEMBRINI (eds.), *Emilio Pucci*, catalogue of the exhibition, "Il Tempo e la Moda," Florence Biennale, Florence, Palazzo Pitti, September 21-December 15, 1996. Milan: Skira, 1996.

ROSITA LEVI-PISETZKY, *Il costume e la moda nella società italiana*. Turin: Einaudi, 1978.

GILLES LIPOVETSKY, *L'Empire de l'éphémère, la mode et son destin dans les sociétés modernes*. Paris: Gallimard, 1987; Engl. ed. *The Empire of Fashion: Dressing Modern Democracy*, trans. by Catherine Porter. Princeton: Princeton University Press, 19994.

STÉPHANE MALLARMÉ, *La dernière mode, Gazzetta del Bel Mondo e della Famiglia*. Milan: Edizioni delle Donne, 1979.

MICHEL MAFFESOLI, *Au creux des apparences. Pour une éthique de l'esthétique*. Paris: Plon, 1990.

GIANNINO MALOSSI (ed.), *La sala Bianca: Nascita della moda italiana*. Milan: Electa, 1992.

MARYA MANNES, "Italian Fashion," in *Vogue*, January 1, 1947.

GIANNA MANZINI, *La moda di Vanessa*, ed. by Nicoletta Campanella. Palermo: Sellerio, 2003.

–, "La moda è una cosa seria," in *La Donna*, July 1935.

–, "Il bianco nella moda," in *Bellezza*, no. 5 (1941).

VINICIO MARINUCCI, "Vetrine," in *Bellezza*, no. 35 (1943).

CLAUDIO MARRA, *Nelle ombre di un sogno. Storia e idee della fotografia di moda*. Milan: Bruno Mondadori, 2004.

RICHARD MARTIN, *Fashion and Surrealism*. London: Thames and Hudson, 1996.

MARSHALL MCLUHAN, "Fashion is the Medium," in *Harper's Bazaar*, April 1968.

ORNELLA MORELLI, "Il successo internazionale della moda italiana e l'esordio in patria del made in Italy postbellico," in Gloria Bianchino, Grazietta Butazzi, Alessandra Mottola Molfino, Arturo Carlo Quintavalle (eds.), *La moda italiana*, vol. I: *Le origini dell'Alta Moda e la maglieria*. Milan: Electa, 1987

ENRICA MORINI, *Storia della moda XVIII-XX*. Milan: Skira, 2000.

EUGENIA PAULICELLI, *Fashion under Fascism*. Oxford-New York: Berg, 2004.

GIO PONTI, "È superfluo il superfluo?" in *Bellezza*, no. 1 (1945).

CAROLINE RENNOLDS MILBANK, *New York Fashion, The Evolution of American Style*. New York: Harry N. Abrams, Inc., 1989.

ELSA ROBIOLA, "Atto di fede," in *Bellezza*, no. 1 (1945).

–, "America insegna," in *Bellezza*, no. 11 (1956).

LUIGI SETTEMBRINI, "From Haute Couture to Prêt-à-porter," in Germano Celant (ed. by), *Italian Metamorphosis 1943-1968*. New York: Guggenheim, 1994.

GEORG SIMMEL, "Fashion," (1904) in D. Levine (ed. by), *Georg Simmel*. Chicago: University of Chicago Press, 1971; It. ed., *La Moda*. Milan: Bruno Mondadori, 1996.

VALERIE STEELE, *Fashion Italian Style*. New Haven-London: Yale University Press, 2003.

–, "Italian Fashion and America," in Germano Celant (ed. by), *Italian Metamorphosis 1943-1968*. New York: Guggenheim, 1994.

–, "Retro Fashion," in *Artforum*, December 1990.

BERNARDO VALLI, BENEDETTA BARZINI, PATRIZIA CALEFATO (eds.), *Discipline della moda. L'etica dell'apparenza*. Naples: Liguori Editore, 2003.

GUIDO VERGANI, *Dizionario della moda*. Milan: Baldini&Castoldi, 1999.

DIANA VREELAND, *D.V.* New York: Da Capo Press, 1997.

NICOLA WHITE, *Reconstructing Italian Fashion: America and the Development of Italian Fashion Industry*. Oxford-New York: Berg, 2000.

ELIZABETH WILSON, *Adorned in Dreams: Fashion and Modernity*. London: Virago, 1985.

EDNA WOOLMAN CHASE, *Always In Vogue*. London: Victor Gollancz, 1954.

## WORKS OF A GENERAL CHARACTER:

ALBERTO ABRUZZESE, *La bellezza per te e per me*. Milan: Bompiani, 1998.

ALBERTO ARBASINO, *Fratelli d'Italia*. Milan: Adelphi, 1993.

–, *Le piccole vacanze*. Turin, Einaudi, 1971.

ALBERTO ASOR ROSA, "La cultura," in *Storia d'Italia*, vol. XIV: *Dall'Unità a Oggi, 2*. Turin: Einaudi, 1975.

ROLAND BARTHES, *La Chambre claire: Note sur la photographie*. Paris: Gallimard, 1980; Engl. ed. *Camera Lucida: Reflections on Photography*, trans. by Richard Howard. New York, Hill and Wang, 1981.

–, *Le Bruissement de la langue*. Paris: Seuil, 1984; Engl. ed., *The Rustle of Language*, trans. by Richard Howard. New York: Hill and Wang, 1986.

–, *Mythologies*. Paris: Seuil, 1957; Engl. ed. *Mythologies*, trans. by Annette Lavers. New York: Hill and Wang, 1984.

–, *Scritti*, Torino, Einaudi, 1998

CHARLES BAUDELAIRE, *Selected Writings on Art and Artists*, trans. by P.E. Charvet. Cambridge: Cambridge University Press, 1988.

WALTER BENJAMIN, "Paris, Capital of the Nineteenth Century. Exposé of 1939," in Id., *The Arcades Project*. London-Cambridge: Belknap/Harvard University Press. 1999.

–, *The Work of Art in the Age of Mechanical Reproduction*. New York: Schocken Books, 1968.

JOHN BERGER, *About Looking*. London: Writers and Readers Publishing Cooperative, 1980.

GIAN PIERO BRUNETTA (ed. by), *Identità italiana e identità europea nel cinema italiano dal 1945 al miracolo economico*. Turin: Edizioni della Fondazione Agnelli, 1996.

JUDITH BUTLER, *Gender Trouble: Feminism and the Subversion of Identity*. London-New York: Routledge, 1990.

ROGER CAILLOIS, "Mimétisme et Psychasténie," in *Minotaure*, no. 7, June 1935.

COLIN CAMPBELL, *The Romantic Ethic and the Spirit of Modern Consumerism*. Oxford-New York: Blackwell, 1987.

EMILIO CECCHI, *America amara*. Padua: Franco Muzzio Editore, 1995.

CAMILLA CEDERNA, *Il lato debole*, ed. by Giulia Borgese and Anna Cederna. Milan: Feltrinelli, 2000.

GERMANO CELANT (ed. by), *The Italian Metamorphosis 1943-1968*. New York: Guggenheim, 1994.

MICHEL DE CERTEAU, *L'invention du quotidien*. Paris: Union Générale d'Editions, 1980; Engl. ed. *The Practice of Everyday Life*, trans. by Steven Rendall. Berkeley: University of California Press, 1984.

ALBA DE CESPEDES, "Eva e le piume," in *Bellezza*, no. 5 (1941).

VANNI CODELUPPI, *Il potere del consumo*. Turin: Bollati Boringhieri, 2003.

GUY DEBORD, *La Société du spectacle*. Paris: Buchet-Chastel, 1967; Engl. ed. *The Society of the Spectacle*, trans. by Donald Nicholson-Smith. New York: Zone Books, 1994.

MICHELA DE GIORGIO, *Le italiane dall'Unità a oggi*. Rome-Bari: Laterza, 1992.

GEORGES DUBY, MICHELLE PERROT (eds.), *L'Histoire des femmes en Occident, de l'Antiquité à nos jours*. Paris: Plon, 1992; Engl. ed. *A History of Women in the West*. London-Cambridge: Harvard University Press, 1992.

UMBERTO ECO, *Apocalittici e integrati*. Milan: Bompiani, 2001.

MAURIZIO FAGIOLO DELL'ARCO (ed. by), *Roma 1948-1959: Arte, cronaca, cultura dal neorealismo alla dolce vita*. Milan: Skira, 2002.

JANET FLANNER, *Paris Was Yesterday (1925-1939)*. New York: Popular Library, 1968.

–, *Uncollected Writings 1932-1975*, ed. by Irving Drutman. New York-London, Harvest/HBJ, 1981.

MICHEL FOUCAULT, "Des espaces autres," in Id., *Dits et écrits*, ed. by Daniel Defert and François Ewald. Paris: Gallimard, 1994, vol. IV.

SILVIA FRANCHINI, SIMONETTA SOLDANI (eds.), *Donne e Giornalismo. Percorsi e presenze di una storia di genere*. Milan: Franco Angeli, 2004.

GÉRARD GENETTE, *Figures II*. Paris, Seuil, 1966.

CHRISTOPH GRUNENBERG, MAX HOLLEIN (eds.), *Shopping*, catalogue of the exhibition, *Shopping. A Century of Art and Consumer Culture*. Ostfildern-Ruit: Hatje Cantz Publishers, 2002.

HANK KAUFMAN, GENE LERNER, *Hollywood sul Tevere*. Milan: Sperling & Kupfer Editore, 1982.

SIEGFRIED KRACAUER, *Das Ornament der Masse* (1927). Frankfurt: Suhrkamp, 1974; Engl. ed. *The Mass Ornament: Weimar Essays*, trans. by Thomas Y. Levin. Cambridge: Harvard University Press, 1995.

ROSALIND KRAUSS, *Le Photographique. Pour une théorie des écarts*. Paris: Macula, 1990.

JACQUES LACAN, *Le séminaire, Livre XI: Les quatre concepts fondamentaux de la psychanalyse*, ed. by Jacques-Alain Miller. Paris: Seuil, 1973; Engl. ed. *Book XI: The Four Fundamental Concepts of Psychoanalysis*, ed. by Jacques-Alain Miller. New York: Norton, 1978.

GIACOMO LEOPARDI, "Zibaldone, Dialogo della Moda e della Morte," in *Tutte le Opere*. Florence: Sansoni, 1969, 2 vols.

ANITA LOOS, *Gentlemen Prefer Blondes* (1925). London: Penguin 20th Century Classics, 1998.

MARSHALL MCLUHAN, *Understanding Media: The Extensions of Man*. New York: New American Library, 1964; repr. Cambridge (MA): MIT Press, 1994.

–, *The Interior Landscape: The Literary Criticism of Marshall McLuhan 1943-1962*, ed. by Eugene McNamara. Toronto: McGraw Hill, 1969.

ELISABETTA MONDELLO, *La nuova italiana*. Rome: Editori Riuniti, 1987.

LAURA MULVEY, *Visual and Other Pleasures*, Basingstoke-London: Macmillan, 1989.

ERWIN PANOFSKY, *Three Essays on Style*. Cambridge (MA): MIT Press, 1995.

CESARE PAVESE, *Tra donne sole*. Turin: Einaudi, 1998.

SUSAN SONTAG, *Against Interpretation and Other Essays*. New York: Picador, 2001.

–, *On Photography*. New York: Farrar Straus & Giroux, 1977.

PAUL VALÉRY, *Degas, danse, dessin* (1938). Paris: Gallimard, 1998; Engl. ed. *Degas Dance Drawing*, trans. by Helen Burlin. New York: Lear, 1948.

TENNESSEE WILLIAMS, *The Roman Spring of Mrs. Stone* (1950). New York: Buccaneer Books, 1997.

VIRGINIA WOOLF, *Hours in a Library*. New York: Harcourt, Brace and Co., 1957.

7o  Io dico che l'avvenire si ricorderà di noi.
                                        1936

8o  Potrebbero ben esser meno ridicole
              per attrarre la vostra attenzione?
                    o vi piaccion così?
                                        1946

9o  I cappelli sono l'umore instabile di
              una testa alla moda.
                                        1947